"CHRISTIANITY IS EVERYBODY'S FULL-TIME BUSINESS,"

according to one of America's most popular religious authors.

YOUR OTHER VOCATION

HARPER JUBILEE BOOKS

YOUR OTHER VOCATION

BY

ELTON TRUEBLOOD

Professor of Philosophy
Earlham College

HARPER & ROW, PUBLISHERS

New York, Hagerstown, San Francisco, London

Library of Congress Catalogue Card Number: 52-11078
ISBN: 0-06-068769-X

75 76 77 78 79 10 9 8 7 6 5 4 3 2 1

To

My Mother
whose vocation
has influenced mine

Contents

Preface

A PHENOMENON familiar to students of intellectual history is that of the growth of a movement from several independent sources at the same time. We are today witnessing a contemporary example of such a phenomenon in the rising tide of interest in *lay religion*. We are witnesses to a movement which crosses all lines of faith or denomination, which is known by many different names, and which appears in several different nations at once, without the benefit of a concerted plan.

It is now desirable that this movement, which, if rightly developed, holds such promise for our day, should have the advantage of all the thought and care which we can muster. We must understand its significance, its dangers, its hope. We must do all we can to make it the redemptive movement of our time which it is capable of becoming. Accordingly as many as possible, who can give the required time and thought, ought to share their careful thinking on this subject with one another. This small book is a modest beginning in such a direction.

The incentive for writing the book is owed to many persons, including the officers and members of The Layman's Movement for a Christian World, but my greatest incentive came when I was asked to deliver the Perkins Lectures at Wichita Falls, Texas, in March of 1952. It was decided to make the topic of this book the topic of the Perkins Lectures. My special thanks go to Mr. and Mrs. J. J. Perkins who founded the lectureship, to Alfred Freeman, and to those who, by transcribing the lectures, made the work of preparing this volume less burdensome.

E. T.

Earlham College
June, 1952

YOUR OTHER VOCATION

CHAPTER I

A Place to Begin

Sooner or later the idea which I here put forward
will conquer the world, for with inexorable logic it
carries with it the intellect as well as the heart.
                                        ALBERT SCHWEITZER

TO TELL the truth is never easy, for the truth is
nearly always complex. Truth telling is particularly
difficult when we try to judge the current scene in the
life of the West, because the tendencies are conflicting
as well as varied. Ours is undoubtedly a dark time, but
to say that and to say no more is to distort the truth, since
ours is also an amazingly bright time. There is widespread
corruption, but there is also a most heartening resurgence
of thought and action *against* the corruption. Millions
live self-indulgent, undisciplined lives, and even meaningless lives, but, in the midst of this, is the appearance of a
neo-Puritanism as a sign, not only of moral recovery, but
also of intellectual maturity. On the one hand, there is
widespread loss of Christian conviction, but, on the other
hand, there is the appearance of new Christian movements
of astonishing vigor.

Part of the paradox of our time lies in the fact that the

good news arises, in large measure, from the realistic facing of the bad news. Our chief gains now come from the courageous ways of reacting to our losses. The strategy of wisdom consists in knowing so well the location of the points at which we are hard pressed that we concentrate our forces on these points and thereby actually turn defeat into victory.

In no part of our culture is the paradoxical combination of loss and gain more striking than at the spiritual center of our common life, the Christian cause. Perhaps there are always both losses and gains, but in our time both have been accentuated fantastically. The perennial situation is, no doubt, that of Ephesus in which the Apostle found, at the same moment, "A wide open door" and "many adversaries,"[1] but in our day the door is extra wide and the adversaries are unusually successful. The Christian gains of our generation are many, and some of them will be mentioned in this book, but it is the part of wisdom to concentrate attention first of all upon our dangers and our losses. In any case this procedure helps to keep us honest and to avoid the self-delusion of easy optimism.

The gravity of the loss to Christendom which the current revolution in China entails is now beginning to dawn upon our people. For the Christian movement to be forced underground throughout many parts of a nation of four hundred fifty million people, itself the chief nation of the modern missionary movement, is sobering indeed.

We understand the gravity of this loss when we contrast the violently anti-Christian mood of the present political

[1] Cor. 16:9.

leaders of China with the mood of the leaders thirty years ago. The late Henry T. Hodgkin, who knew the older China so well, mentioned, in 1919, the contrast between India and China in regard to Christianity. After recognizing the anti-Christian sentiment of many Indian leaders, he continued, "In China, on the other hand, many of the finer spirits in the revolutionary movement have been and are Christians, and not a few who do not call themselves Christians recognise that Christ is the one in whom China has most hope of realising her deepest aspirations toward progress and democracy."[2]

It would be hard to find another statement which could make us realize so vividly the extent of our spiritual setback. But, serious as the defeat in China may be, the loss in the heart of the West is serious too. Our Western losses are, of course, not as dramatic, but they are nevertheless real. Though our Western civilization is still nominally Christian, the living connection with our Christian roots is, at various points, very slight, while at others the connection seems actually to be severed. Many phases of our culture are like the provinces of the later Roman Empire, in which the forms of Roman sovereignty were retained, though the provinces were in reality lost. When the barbarians came these provinces fell easily, with almost no struggle.

Today we are faced with the fact that there are lost provinces of the Christian faith all around us. One of these, of which we are vividly conscious, is labor. In the early

[2] Henry T. Hodgkin, *Lay Religion* (London: The Swarthmore Press, 1919), p. 85 n.

days of our American experiment the people who worked with their hands were as consciously loyal to the Christian cause as were the professional classes, but this is certainly not the situation in the middle of the twentieth century. About half of the residents of the United States are claimed as church members, but it is well known that, in many areas, the church is now looked upon as an upper-class institution. There are large churches without a single member who also belongs to a labor union. The characteristic supporters of the Christian movement are white collar workers, managers, professional people and farmers. The gravity of the loss is made vivid by the fact that, in some cities, meetings of labor unions are now held in labor "temples" at eleven o'clock on Sunday mornings. In short, the province of labor is so far lost that, far from thinking of itself as a part of the Christian movement, it has set itself up as a genuine rival, in the competition for loyalty.

There is no doubt that this loss is very great. The sense of its seriousness is accentuated by the recognition of the degree to which the earlier labor movement was so largely inspired by conscious Christian motivation. Men, with the theology of Walter Rauschenbusch to buttress them, became union organizers in an effort to make Christian ideals prevail, but little of this connection now remains. There are a few union leaders, like the Reuther brothers, who are consciously associated with the Christian cause, but such men now constitute a tiny minority. One consequence is a general loss of idealism, with the frank acceptance of a sordid struggle for power.

Another province now largely lost is that of education.

It is well known that the characteristic American college, a truly unique cultural contribution of our particular nation, was originally founded by consciously Christian planning and sacrifice. It is not an exaggeration to say that a majority of these institutions have now been severed from their roots, while some are centers of sheer paganism. The chapel may still stand in the middle of the quadrangle, but it is only in a geographical sense that it is central; in every other sense it is *peripheral*. What is really central is the basketball court or the ballroom floor or the technological laboratory. We know how far we have moved in the direction of secularism when we realize that the picture of Yale, dominated by the powerful Christian mentality of Timothy Dwight, now seems quaint.

There are institutions which have never renounced, on paper, their Christian connection, but in practice are almost wholly pagan. Their leaders are afraid to take a forthright Christian stand, for fear that they might thus seem to lose their position of academic "objectivity," and they give advancement to instructors who take advantage of their positions by ridiculing whatever faith their young students may have. At the same time a sentimental reference to the Christian *background* is still printed in the catalogue.

The gravity of this loss is something which it is almost impossible to exaggerate. Christian forces once controlled these institutions of enormous potentiality and then slowly *gave them away*. In most cases the loss of this province has been made to appear in the guise of virtue. The institutions were supposedly "liberated," but the consequent freedom is not always attractive or beneficent to anyone concerned. In many situations all that is achieved by the liberation is the "freedom" of a ship which has lost both anchor and rudder and consequently drifts, the victim of any wind that blows. Great scientific work is done by humble and honest men in most institutions of higher learning, but these men are often deeply discouraged by the degree to which the institutions they serve have become places of luxurious and meaningless lounging, in a situation almost wholly devoid of a sense of greatness. As the province of higher education has been lost, it has moved in the direction of pretentious triviality.

A parallel loss has gone on in our lower schools, where the secularization of our children's school books has been carried out so rigorously, and with such thoroughness, that an outsider, in looking at them, might not even suspect that our civilization once had a Christian basis at all. We have moved a long way from the time when *McGuffey's Readers* could include, without apology to anyone, a versified form of the Ten Commandments. It is important to add, however, that in both the schools and the colleges a reverse movement is beginning to appear. It is highly significant that several strong colleges have, in the last few years, made a deliberate effort to recover their heritage, while a few have announced a program that is unapologetically Christian. At the same time the National Education Association has made a strong emphasis on moral recovery and, through its official publications, has stressed the necessity of a vigorous and intelligent religious commitment. It is in such ways that the items of bad news and of good news are mixed.

One of the chief reasons why a change is setting in, so far as lower and higher education are concerned, is the pragmatic one that the results achieved by severing the cultural roots are not really attractive. In eliminating the Christian center of our education we soon found that we had eliminated much else at the same time. It is no accident that some of the worst examples of corruption during the past two years have come, not in government or business, but in *colleges*. The pagan philosophy is not really so appealing, when it is applied with logical consistency. The substitution of the stadium for the chapel, as the focal point of education, is not an unqualified success.

Another province which is largely lost, so far as the Christian faith is concerned, is that of the intellectuals. It is a striking fact that so many of the intellectual fads and fancies of our time have been logically incompatible with a vital Christianity. If they are true, then the gospel is false. Characteristic movements, marked by this radical incompatibility, are *behaviorism* in psychology, *ethical subjectivism* in sociological thinking, *mechanistic philosophy* in some branches of natural science and *logical positivism* in all areas of thought.

The Christian faith, of course, has nothing to fear from these movements if they can be met openly. It is still true, as it was in the *ancient* pagan world, that Christians can outthink as well as outlive their opponents, but many of our contemporary intellectuals have not even bothered to face the kind of thinking which Christianity has produced in such abundance in our amazing generation. Assuming, ignorantly, that the faith is a matter of mere feeling, without intellectual content, they avoid the contact of mind with mind and go on blissfully. They know, in a dim way, that outstanding intellectuals like Emil Brunner, Jacques Maritain, T. S. Eliot and Reinhold Niebuhr are deeply committed Christians, but since they cannot really believe that this is possible, they pay no attention.

The influence of Reinhold Niebuhr is the source of important insights into our contemporary mentality. He draws great crowds wherever he goes, particularly in academic centers, but the spectacle seems to the majority somehow fantastic. It is like that of a dog walking on his hind legs, something to be shrugged off as a curious exception. How can a man so obviously intelligent actually believe in such old-fashioned ideas as the divinity of Christ and original sin? For most of those who listen, the accumulated academic prejudices are so deep and so numerous that they cannot give open-minded attention to the argument. In a brilliant review of Professor Niebuhr's latest book, *The Irony of American History,* Crane Brinton, after a highly appreciative estimate of the thinking included in the book, ends on a note of deep questioning, so far as the contemporary intellectual scene is concerned. The reviewer writes:

The fascinating question which Dr. Niebuhr's life work suggests is whether our "liberals," "progressives," "non-communist Left"—call them what you will, they are identifiable enough perhaps in this country by the term "intellectuals"—

can really adopt, not necessarily Dr. Niebuhr's Christian theism, which would for many of them be an impossible wrenching from the positivist strata two centuries have filled in around them, but even his pessimistic view of human nature.[3]

Here is a really arresting phrase, "the positivistic strata two centuries have filled in around them." There is no doubt that these impediments exist and that, if a Christian civilization is to flourish, they must be removed or made less restrictive to free thought. The Christian faith cannot survive and be effective unless it can present a coherent picture of reality which faces all of the serious difficulties and surmounts them better than does any alternative system of belief. Much of our problem has been involved in the fact that so many of our supposed intellectuals have been so naïve in their positivistic faith that they have not even recognized the inconsistencies of their own system, let alone its inadequacy to do justice to the full richness of human experience.

In this, as in the case of other lost provinces, however, there is today some hope. The hope lies chiefly in the way in which a good many, who have heretofore been complacently satisfied, are now disturbed and thus begin to be genuine seekers. Insofar as they are really intelligent,

[3] Crane Brinton, "The Problem of Human Evil in History," *New York Herald Tribune, Book Review*, April 6, 1952, p. 5. A partial verification of Crane Brinton's judgment is provided by the review of the same book in *The New Yorker*. In striking contrast to what we normally expect to find in this valuable magazine, the review of the new Niebuhr book shows a curious failure to understand. The reviewer even fails to distinguish between the Christian understanding of man and ordinary pessimism.

and not merely pretentious in their claims, they are forced
to realize that our experiment in paganism has not been a
success. There is always hope when men are roused out
of their dogmatic slumbers. A particularly vivid demonstration of that hope is shown in the lives of a number of
mature men and women who have been driven to a vital
faith, not by the denial of thought, but by the fuller
acceptance of it. Characteristic conversions are those of
Professor Chad Walsh of Beloit College, James Pike,
recently of Columbia University and now Dean of the
Cathedral of St. John the Divine, and Will Herberg,
whose book *Judaism and Modern Man* exposes pitilessly
the ambiguities of the nonreligious intellectual. Here, too,
the existence of vicious adversaries and the open door are
compatible aspects of our current scene.

The significance of these lost provinces, in relation to
out total predicament, must be carefully understood. Why
give serious thought to these intellectual matters, asks the
ordinary citizen, when everyone knows that we are threat-
ened by Russian Communism? What we need to do, says
this plain man as he reads the morning paper, is to build
up our armed forces, increase our technological strength,
win in Korea and drive those sympathetic with Communism out of our own government.

The chief weakness of this familiar line of argument is
that if it were taken seriously, as a sufficient policy, the
world struggle could easily become nothing more than a
contest of power. On this basis we might become quite
as totalitarian as our enemy and, if that should ever occur,
the outcome of the power struggle would thereby become

a matter of indifference. We shall not be saved by power alone, for power is intrinsically untrustworthy; it can be used for cruel ends quite as effectively as for beneficent ends. What makes the greatest difference is the core of conviction at the center of our life, in the interest of which power is supposedly employed.

We have a dim consciousness of the necessity of this core of conviction, but the expression of this consciousness in our contemporary scene is almost wholly negative. We spend our nights and days telling how bad the communist creed is and how bad the communist leaders are. In all this we are undoubtedly correct, but such a stand does not give us an adequate basis of living. That will not come except by the development of an affirmative and positive conviction.

In order to develop an affirmative faith we must present and demonstrate a conception of human life that is more exciting and more appealing, especially to the submerged peoples of the earth, than the one which now dominates minds beyond the curtain. In short, there is no chance for us unless we have a *gospel*, but a gospel is what we are most inept in producing. We find it far more difficult to produce than a new machine, a bomb or a football formation, partly because the very idea of a gospel is slightly embarrassing. Only the do-gooder has a gospel and who, in America, wants to be known as a do-gooder? An idealist is almost as unpopular as a fellow traveler.

We can go our present way for a while if we prefer it, but, if so, we shall be weaker every succeeding day. Often our weakness will be hidden from us, because we may show scattered symptoms of success for several years. We may fill the various bowls with spectators; we may build up a very large army and a truly formidable air force and we may overlook the inevitable inflationary results, because we shall have some of the external marks of prosperity. But no matter how skillfully we hide our weakness, it will exist, and finally some severe strain will reveal it. The deep and awful truth is the Biblical proposition, "Where there is no vision the people perish."

Fortunately, we do not need to conjure up a new vision. We are not waiting for some latter-day Karl Marx, sitting in the British Museum and dreaming up a new scheme of human society. We *have* a scheme and what we need is men and women of all walks of life who will dedicate their energies to its recovery and fulfillment. The prelude to an affirmative vision, without which we shall perish, is a recovery of the revolutionary appeal of the Christian faith. This is not the end of the matter, but it is a practical place to start. We must have millions who give their nights and days to the effort to understand our affirmative answer and to make it win by its own inherent appeal.

What we need is a burning and passionate faith to which we can give ourselves. We cannot do much about the other side of the iron curtain, but we can do a good deal about *this* side and the need here is apparent. The contrast which exists between our lethargy and the burning zeal of the young leaders of China is sobering to contemplate. Though we make commencement speeches about democracy, we certainly are not aroused about it as the young communists are aroused by Marx-Leninism. The difference lies in the fact that democracy, as we ordinarily understand it, is little more than a political system, whereas Marx-Leninism is vastly more; it is a religion. Only a religion can arouse men and women as we need to be aroused and the only religion which has the slightest chance of performing the required miracle is a revitalized form of the Judeo-Christian faith, which has proved its ability to save men and civilizations in other times of crisis in nearly two thousand years of troubled history. The basic Christian faith, shorn of its denominational impediments, is, in sober truth, the only known force that is more than a match for the passionate zeal which the Marxian gospel has been able to inspire during the past thirty-five years. A revitalized faith would not save us from strain, but it might enable us to live nobly in the midst of the strain.

What is so sobering to us is the recognition that even this faith, which is literally our only hope, shows so many signs of dullness and decay. The salt, which was designed to preserve the world from decay, has not wholly lost its saltness, but in many areas it has been so adulterated that little effectiveness is in evidence. The early Christians, who had been severely beaten and admonished to keep quiet, proceeded with their public and private witness without the loss of a single day,[4] but their modern successors are satisfied if they go to church on Easter.

As we face the loss of whole provinces, now separated from the kingdom of Christ, our first problem is one of strategy. Obviously, if we care, we shall refuse to sit down complacently under the present situation or satisfy our-

[4] Acts 5:42.

selves by continuing to convince the already convinced. *The provinces must be rewon.* What we must do is to regroup our forces and to make our attack at the points where attack is possible or where there is a fair chance of success. No serious Christian will apologize for using military metaphors; the New Testament abounds in them.

In our strategy of renewal we can gain wisdom from an analysis of former experiences, in other centuries, when losses were correspondingly great. It is heartening to realize that the loss of faith seemed almost complete when Joseph Butler started to write *The Analogy of Religion* and that the whole temper of the people was radically altered by the end of his century. There was almost no Christian conviction among the students of Yale when Timothy Dwight began his famous presidency, but such conviction was practically universal when he ended his career.

One of the most illuminating experiences of recovery is that inaugurated by Ignatius Loyola when he founded the Society of Jesus four hundred years ago. Loyola saw his beloved Church losing out on every side. Nearly all of northern Europe had seceded in the Reformation, while, in southern Europe, there was widespread corruption and apathy. Loyola proposed to form a disciplined band dedicated to the recovery of the lost provinces. It was a commando group, made up of individuals who might be called upon, with short notice, to fight on any front. As all the world knows, this order has been enormously successful and remains so to this day. The principle, applied by Loyola to the recovery of a single church, can be applied to the recovery of Basic Christianity, without reference to denominational lines of affiliation or loyalty.

This gives us our lead for the major recovery of the lost provinces; it can provide our generation with a wholly new conception of what it means to be a Christian. We must form a *new order*, devoted to such recovery, each member finding the sector where he can fight best and each strengthened by the realization of what others are doing in other sectors. Some must dedicate themselves to the recovery of the ranks of labor, some to the bringing back of a sense of meaning in the colleges, some to reaching the intellectuals and some to still other enterprises of a similar nature. All can feel that the enterprise is a single one, even though individuals give themselves to lonely and widely separated assignments.

The task before the new order of our time is not merely that of recovery, but also that of advance, because, if we are not going forward, we are already in decay. In the long run the only sound defense is *attack*. In order to attack we must find where our unused human resources are and learn to employ them in the struggle. Our strategy is to find new areas into which the fundamental Christian insights can penetrate and thus change the world. There is no good reason why the words of the risen Lord, "Go, ʃe, into all the world," may not be taken *intensively* as well as *extensively*. Usually we have interpreted this injunction in a geographical sense, but there is a deeper significance, according to which they may mean that all phases of life, economic, political, cultural and domestic, must be deeply penetrated. If our new order is to succeed in the recovery of the lost provinces it must be a society of penetrators in common life, not people separated from it.

Almost every community in the Western world has many reminders of the Christian heritage in the presence of ecclesiastical buildings, and in some of these buildings significant events occur, but not in all. There is a great deal of good preaching and some of it is actually brilliant, but the shame is that most of it reaches the wrong people because it is heard only by people who already believe what they are being told. A great proportion of current preaching is merely a convincing of the already convinced, while the masses outside are almost wholly untouched.

If, in this situation, one truth is more obvious than any other, it is that *we cannot win except by a radical change.* If all we have to offer is the tame routine of the conventional church, with slight improvements in technique, we might as well give up. The modern church will not make a sufficient difference by a slight improvement in the anthems or by a little better preaching or by a little better organization of the Sunday Schools. Many of these are fairly good already, but not much seems to happen, so far as the pagan order is concerned. Those cities with the worst political corruption have no dearth of church buildings. It is sobering to be reminded that Rome, when the city fell into such moral and political decay, shortly before the Gothic attack, had more than four hundred shrines. It is equally sobering and truly humbling to a Christian to realize that the present racial policy in South Africa has been promoted by a prime minister who claims, perhaps sincerely, to be motivated by the Christian faith. It is no wonder that the seeker is often confused by what he sees.

What we need is a radical change of some kind. The parable that applies to our situation is the contemporary parable of the *big dose,* according to which some of the modern wonder drugs must be given in very large amounts in order for them to make a *sufficient* difference. Often the small dose is entirely wasted, because the body adjusts rapidly to it. In some medication, if we do not give a large dose, we might as well give none. Not only must the dose be big; it must also be new. The reason for this is that so many have already failed to be moved by present means. We have done about all we can do unless we find a new approach. It must be an approach which gives a practical means of service to the many humble people who are really eager to help, but do not now know what to do. There is actually a great deal of good will and a vast store of decency, but the problem is to harness this good will in some effective manner. In nearly every community there are hundreds of people who are sincerely eager to do something to help to produce a better world, but they do not know what to do. All of the problems seem so large that any effort appears futile and therefore nothing is done. What we need is a *handle.* Where can it be found?

So far as the Christian faith is concerned the practical handle in our time is lay religion. If in the average church we should suddenly take seriously the notion that every lay member, man or woman, is really a minister of Christ, we could have something like a revolution in a very short time; it would constitute both the big dose and the required novelty. Suddenly the number of ministers in the average church would jump from *one* to *five hundred*. This is the way to employ valuable but largely wasted human resources. The change that could come in the visitation of new families, in the spoken and written word, and in public witness might be incalculably great. In a few communities, where the idea has been seriously tried, the change has already been encouragingly great.

Let no one have the temerity to say that this is what we already have. It is not! There are thousands of contemporary churches in which nothing of the kind is even *understood*, let alone demonstrated. Most Protestants pay lip service to the Reformation doctrine of the priesthood of every believer, but they do not thereby mean to say that every Christian is a minister. Many hasten to add that all they mean by the familiar doctrine is that nobody needs to confess to a priest, since each can confess directly to God. The notion that this doctrine erases the distinction between laymen and minister is seldom presented seriously, and would, to some, be shocking, but it does not take much study of the New Testament to realize that the early Christians actually operated on this revolutionary basis.

How far we have departed from the New Testament practice may be shown by describing a contemporary Christian gathering, the example being taken almost at random. The gathering was organized to strengthen the Protestant forces of the city, a speaker being brought from a distance. The entire affair was conducted by the local ministerial association, one pastor giving the invocation, one reading the Scripture, another praying before the offering, a fourth introducing the speaker and a fifth giving the benediction. The whole service was practically identical with that which most of the attenders had experienced earlier the same day, except that the professional participants were now more numerous. There was no surprise, no novelty, no real beauty or dignity, and consequently very little attention. It was as though an old record, worn by much use, were being run again and no one seemed to have any clear reason for running it. The hymns were sung, not because some great testimony was being jointly made, but because hymn singing was the conventional thing to do, and the prayers were given, not because of inner compulsion, but because praying was expected.

On the platform all were professionals. There was not a layman, not a woman, not a young person. In the congregation sat about two hundred people, *one* of whom was possibly under twenty-one years of age! This seems shocking, and means defeat, but why should we consider it surprising? What was there to draw the young or the adventurous? Even if they *had* been present, they would have been expected to play the role of spectators or mere audience, watching the professionals perform. Thus the mood of the spectator, which is so destructive of any vital movement, is actually encouraged.

The First Reformation which came to its climax more than three centuries ago produced a great new power, by something analagous to a change of gears. As we look back now on that marvelous and rapid development, which did so much to bring democracy to our world, we realize that the crucial step was that of making available the open

Bible. That is why, so far as the English-speaking world is concerned, the key date is 1611. In the intervening three hundred and forty years we have come to take so much for granted the availability of the Bible to the ordinary Christian that we have little understanding how different life was when the Bible was available only to the learned, and to the priestly caste. The Bible, being a revolutionary document, is naturally an instrument of emancipation. The men and women, who could read the Bible for themselves and thus begin to understand God's will directly, soon developed a radical democracy in church government, and, once they had experience in democratic church government, they were not satisfied without democracy in secular government. Thus democratic practices arose simultaneously on two sides of the Atlantic in the small devout communities, especially those of the nonconformist variety.

Now, after more than three centuries, we can, if we will, change gears again. Our opportunity *for a big step lies in opening the ministry to the ordinary Christian in much the same manner that our ancestors opened Bible reading to the ordinary Christian.* To do this means, in one sense, the inauguration of a new Reformation while in another it means the logical completion of the earlier Reformation in which the implications of the position taken were neither fully understood nor loyally followed.

There have been different great steps at different times in Christian history, because one of the most remarkable features of the Christian faith is its ability to reform itself *from the inside.* However vigorous the outside critics of the Church may be, the inside critics, who love the movement which they criticize, are far more vigorous and searching. Reformation is not accidental or exceptional, but characteristic and intrinsic. The crust forms repeatedly, but there is always volcanic power to break through it.

In the nineteenth century the Church experienced a marvelous reformation in the sudden and explosive growth of the missionary movement. Many aspects of Christian life were radically changed in this way and young people went out by the thousands to the ends of the earth. This was a proud and glorious chapter in Christian history and it is by no means ended, but the first impact of this movement is over. Indeed, after years of expansion, we have suffered *reverses*. We still sing, "Jesus shall reign," but we are well aware that the missionary movement now faces terrible obstacles, particularly in China, where most of the Western workers are not allowed to remain and where many of the Chinese converts have, under heavy pressure, renounced the faith they once espoused.

Now, just as one great chapter of expansion is temporarily ended, another chapter is being inaugurated. This is the chapter devoted to the ministry of the laity. Whether or not this will produce a new reformation we cannot yet know, but we do know that, as has been true in earlier movements, almost identical developments are occurring spontaneously and without knowledge of one another, in a great many different localities. The great Church Congress of Germany, which brought together almost four hundred thousand persons in Berlin in the summer of 1951, was largely inspired by the concept of lay religion and largely organized by a layman, Reinold von Thadden, whose work for the promotion of lay religion has been honored in America. Many conferences on lay religion have been held in 1952 and more are already planned for succeeding years. We have witnessed the organization of "United Church Men," the beginnings of a training school for lay ministers, the spread of the Christopher Movement among Roman Catholics, the growing use of the Yoke-pin, the organization of Presbyterian Men, and much more. Every succeeding week brings new evidence of the vitality of an idea whose time has come.

CHAPTER II

The Revolt of the Laymen

Every great religious awakening has
been a revolt against authority,
HENRY T. HODGKIN

THE growth of lay ministry is one of the important
facts of our puzzling time, though it is neither generally recognized nor well understood. Indeed it is so
little understood that the new phrase "The Ministry of
the Laity" undoubtedly appears to some as a contradiction
in terms, while to others the very word "laity" is puzzling.
It was the original intention to use this phrase as the title
of the present volume, but many advised against it on the
ground that the language would be puzzling to the very
people to whom it was addressed.

Originally, in the New Testament, the term "laity"
meant all of the people in the early Christian movement,
the *laos*, but finally a lay person has come to mean any
nonprofessional, whatever the field under consideration.
Thus we can be laymen regarding medicine, i.e., not
physicians, laymen regarding the Young Men's Christian
Association, i.e., not paid secretaries, laymen regarding
the law, i.e., not trained lawyers, and, finally, laymen re-

garding the Christian cause, i.e., not clergymen. The general assumption, all the more powerful because unstated, is that the position of the layman is the same in each of these situations and that the important work in each field is nearly always done by the professional. The movement of lay religion in our time is, in essence, a conscious and widespread revolt against this tacit assumption.

In order to understand correctly the present revolt of the laymen we need to have a clear picture of the conventional religious pattern against which the revolt is directed. The conventional view is that the situation in religion is parallel to that in medicine. Just as you cannot have hospitals and clinics without doctors, so, it is generally assumed, you cannot have churches without clergymen. Indeed it is widely believed that, in both areas, the professional is the chief operator. Since it seems reasonable to maintain a sharp distinction, in the healing art, between the authorized physician and the untrained amateur, why not, we argue, do the same in our religion?

That this parallelism seems reasonable to many is evident by our practice. We attend a study group of thoughtful adults, men and women in middle life who are engaged in the serious study of serious Christian books. They are trying to take their right places in the acceptance of responsibility, but their practice betrays a strange failure to go the whole way in that acceptance. They think they ought to open the meeting with prayer, which may be a good idea, but they carefully arrange to have this prayer given by the pastor. They apparently consider that he is the right man to do the public praying, just as they consider the surgeon the right man to take out the child's tonsils. The Young Men's Christian Association puts on an annual dinner, with a fine program and with excellent discussion, but the chairman feels it necessary to import a clergyman to give the prayer. When the chairman is asked the reason for this he becomes embarrassed. He ought to feel embarrassed, in the light of the fact that he is surrounded by three hundred men who are devoted Christians, even though they are persons who do not happen to be "ordained." Apparently praying is a highly professionalized job, with which the amateur cannot be trusted. Or is there a fear that the members of the clergy will feel slighted if others take over their prerogatives? In general the confusion arises from lack of serious thought, and is therefore something which careful analysis ought to be able to cure or at least to mitigate.

If, by the ministry, we mean the religious service of our fellow men, it soon becomes clear that this vocation is potentially universal. Not only does it include both sexes and various races; it can also include those who follow a great variety of occupations. John Bunyan was a tinker, Francis of Assisi a soldier and John Woolman a tailor, but it is obvious that all were ministers, because they were persons who *ministered*. They could and did speak to the spiritual condition of their neighbors in remarkably redemptive ways. The ministry of Woolman was not hindered ever so slightly by the fact that he was a tailor, just as the contemporary ministry of J. C. Penney is not hindered by the fact that he is a merchant. It would be very hard for Mr. Penney to be both a merchant and a practicing

physician; but the ministry raises no difficulty in this
regard. Just as one man may be both minister and merchant another may be both minister and physician and
there is no conflict between the two vocations. The vocation of the ministry is thus different from most others in
its lack of exclusiveness.

Healing cannot, in the nature of things, be a universal
vocation, but the ministry *can* be and it is the contention
of the lay movement of our day that it *ought* to be. Whatever a person's ordinary vocation in the world, whether
salesmanship or homemaking or farming, the ministry
can be his other vocation and perhaps his truest vocation.
Most vocations are mutually incompatible, but the ministry is compatible with all others, providing they are productive of human welfare.

A second way in which the ministry is unique is that,
in performing it, the amateur often has advantages which
are denied to the professional practitioner. This is most
clear if we contrast the role of the professional in religion
with the role of the professional in medicine. Medicine is
something which needs to be highly professionalized, because it is so largely a matter of acquired and practiced
skill. The idea of every man as his own surgeon is a mani-
fest absurdity, whereas the idea of every man as a minister
is not absurd at all. There are a good many reasons why I
cannot remove my own appendix or fill the cavities in my
own teeth, but there are no necessary reasons why I may
not meet the Living God in prayer or help my fellow men
to find Him.

We begin to realize how unfounded the common assumption is when we notice that, in many fields, such as natural science, the increased professionalism of the individual makes him *more* trustworthy whereas in the life of religion the increased professionalism may make him *less* trustworthy. In various succeeding centuries it has been necessary for the religious pioneer to oppose the professionals who had been made less sensitive to religious truth by the very acceptance, on the part of others and themselves, of their authoritarian positions. It is well known that Amos and other prophets of Israel had to fight the priests of their day and that Christ, surrounded by his fishermen followers, suffered more from the entrenched religious leaders than from any other class. Similar experiences have come often in Christian history, that of George Fox three hundred years ago being characteristic of many others. This religious revolt against the professionals is part of what Thomas Carlyle had in mind in a dramatic chapter of *Sartor Resartus* called "Greatest Incident in Modern History." This, says Carlyle, came when Fox, the leather worker, started out on his great lay ministry. Fox had the vivid conviction that going to Oxford or Cambridge was not sufficient to make a man a minister.

Though training may have immense advantages, some of which will be discussed in Chapter V, it is important to realize, at the outset, that the amateur in the Christian ministry has certain definite and marked advantages of his own. The first of these is involved in the fact that the lay minister does not have to bear the stigma of being a clergyman. Though anticlericalism is stronger in some countries than others, usually being strongest in those countries which are priest ridden, there is no Western country without it. Often this takes the form, not of open antagonism, but of patronizing regard. The clergyman is usually known as a good person individually, but his work is not really respected and he is often tolerated in a good-natured way.

The countless service and luncheon clubs are so revealing of our culture that they deserve more careful study than they have usually been given. Most of the clubs have one or more clergymen as members, ostensibly because they seek to have representatives of all parts of their communities, but also, it may be surmised, because the presence of the professionally devout man is often convenient. In most clubs the clerical members become the official pray-ers and this adds respectability to the organization. Every clergyman knows what it is to be patronized in such connections. Fellow members frequently announce that they are going "to come to hear him some time," with the obvious conviction that this remark is somehow complimentary.

Most words of a clergyman are minimized simply because he is supposed to say them. A pastor's convictions are discounted because he is supposed to have a professional stake in the effort to make them prevail. Sometimes people sink so low as to remark that this is what he is paid for; he is on the side of the angels by virtue of his employment. The contrast in effect is often enormous when a layman's remarks are taken seriously, even though he says practically the same words. His words are given full weight, not because he is a more able exponent, but because he is wholly free from any stigma of professionalism.

The importance of this contrast is seen vividly in family visitation. It is the recorded experience of various communities that the visitation evangelism of laymen and women is peculiarly effective, whereas a pastor's call on the same people may have had little or no influence. The chief reason for this difference seems to be the deep feeling that the pastor is only doing his required or routine work, whereas the layman's call is a happy surprise. The pastor is supposed to be *for* the church, much as the labor organizer is *for* the union, but the lay worker who makes a call is credited with calling out of genuine conviction, concern or even friendship. The chemist who is preaching a sermon may, if he is well informed, say about the same things that a trained theologian would say, but there are many people who will give him a far closer attention.

This clear advantage of the amateur in the ministry is something we need to recognize with frankness and to consider carefully as we plan the strategy of renewal. In general it is always better to have a sermon given by a layman than by a pastor, providing the lay person can give it equally well, and it is better to have a call made by a layman, providing similar conditions are met. It is better simply because the results are more conducive to the ends sought.

A second advantage held by the lay minister, in contrast with his professional colleague, is that he is often closer to common life. He is already in the factory, the bank or the office, and thus does not need to gain entrance from the outside. Often he does not need to make many calls because he is with fellow workers all day long and able thereby to make his witness to them. The Christian university professor, whatever subject he teaches, has an advantage in Christian work over the denominational counselor, who must knock at the door. The insider, with his amateur standing, has a great opportunity because of his daily contacts in the course of his ordinary duties.

A third advantage possessed by the lay minister is that of a certain freshness. This advantage is not unique to the ministry, but is found in almost all fields of work. The trained expert gains a great deal by his grasp of the inherited wisdom of his craft, but it is always possible, at the same time, that he is blinded, thereby, to possible new ways of doing or thinking. The amateur, not knowing the difficulties, and consequently not being discouraged by them, may perform wonders which the experienced are afraid to try. In all tasks there are some things revealed to babes which are hidden from the wise and prudent. Ignorance of the supposedly impossible may be dangerous, but it *can* be a wonderful asset. The amateur sometimes wins because he is not wise enough to know when he is beaten.

Though the advantages just enumerated would be sufficient to lead concerned people to a new emphasis on the lay ministry, a still stronger incentive is provided by the reconsideration of the power of such ministry in the remarkable victory of early Christianity. The spread of early Christianity was not as rapid as has been the spread of Marx-Leninism in our century, the new world religion of the twentieth century having covered almost half the earth in thirty-five years, but the growth of Christianity was amazing in that it was carried on against fearful odds, without the aid of an army and without the strategy of fear. We need to find the secret of the early Christians and to employ it again.

One of our dangers, in reading the New Testament, is to read the words merely in the light of our own contemporary experience. It is undoubtedly true that many twentieth-century Christians, when they read words like "pastor" or "minister," think of what they know in a modern town, though in fact the earlier connotation was almost entirely different. The contrast between the church at Corinth in the year 52 and the First Congregational Church of Technopolis in 1952 is really enormous. Owning no building, the Corinthian Christians made use of a synagogue and of private homes, including that of Justus. The picture which comes to us with such power is that of a fallible yet devoted group, all of whom were on fire with missionary zeal and all of whom were engaged in the active ministry. All were of the laity in the sense that all were nonprofessional, but all were ministers in the sense that all ministered. Given their faith in Christ, no other situation was possible and the result was that their contagious influence finally penetrated the whole of the ancient world. No part of the culture could be impervious to the powerful influences set up by a society marked by a universal ministry.

There are many contrasts between current Christianity and that of Christ's day, but the limitation of the ministry to a professional class of men is the most shocking of all these contrasts. Today there are church dignitaries, with high-sounding names, but Jesus said, "Call no man Father" and "Be not called Rabbi." The Pauline Letters were addressed to the rank and file of Christians, not merely to prophets or apostles, and they remind all members of their holy "calling." The ordinary member believed that he was *called* to the ministry quite as literally as was the Apostle, for, just as there is *one Lord, one faith* and *one baptism,* there is *one hope of your calling.*

The degree to which an early Christian Church was a confraternity is difficult for us to understand, but we begin to have some inkling of it when we learn that the capacity in which the Roman government seems first to have recognized the Christian brotherhood was in their corporate capacity as burial clubs. The members were responsible for one another's lives in various ways, all sharing in the ministry to all. Tertullian said, "Where three are gathered together, there is a church, even though they be laymen."

How little, in primitive Christianity, the call to the ministry was limited to an especially ordained group is obvious from the careful study of the New Testament epistles. For example, we read in II Corinthians 5:18, "And all things are of God, who hath reconciled us to Himself by Jesus Christ, and hath given to us the ministry of reconciliation." The word "us" is used with the same denotation in both parts of the sentence and the first clearly refers to *all Christians,* since it is not a special class that God has reconciled. Therefore the second use, in regard to the ministry, must also refer to all. The original recipients of the epistle, i.e., "all the saints that are in Achaia," are urged to comport themselves so as to bring no bad reputation on the ministry (II Corinthians 6:3).[1]

This acceptance of the ministry of all, in a radical democracy, did not, so far as early Christians were concerned, involve a dull uniformity or any lack of a division of labor. Like all intelligent democrats, the early Christians understood thoroughly that democracy is compatible with responsible leadership. The formula developed was that, while all are called to be ministers, some are particularly called to be pastors. It is a mark of our present failure even to understand the New Testament conception, that we ordinarily use the words "pastor" and "minister" synonymously or interchangeably.

The mature statement of the primitive Christian pattern of the ministry is given in the fourth chapter of Ephesians. In this statement, an amplification of that in I Corinthians 12:28 ff., there is a frank recognition of a division of labor without any denial of the universality of responsibility. We are missing the early Christian conception, either when we so stress the ministry of all that we neglect the importance of the pastoral office or when

[1] Though the ordinary church member, in most denominations, seems still to miss the great idea that the nonministering Christian was nonexistent in the early Christian pattern, the idea has long been familiar to scholars. The classic work on this subject is that of Bishop J. B. Lightfoot on The Christian Ministry (London: Macmillan & Company, Ltd., 1878). This valuable work is bound with Bishop Lightfoot's commentary on the Epistle to the Philippians. "The only priests under the Gospel," he says, "designated as such in the New Testament, are the saints, the members of the Christian brotherhood."

we so stress the importance of the pastoral office that we deny the ministry of all. The mature statement in Ephesians upholds the necessity of responsible leadership, but the significant factor is the understanding of the function of the leader. *His function is to help to equip the members for the work of the ministry.* The good pastor or teacher is one who cultivates the ministerial possibilities of his fellow members.

A full understanding of this primitive Christian pattern, which proved to be enormously successful, will avoid many dangers in the *release* of new lay forces in our time. It is unfortunately true that there are a few clergymen who resist the fuller participation of laymen in the ministry, because they feel that their own function thereby seems less important, in that they no longer have a monopoly on the work of the ministry. But it is important to report that the pastors who resist the return to the primitive Christian pattern, out of a desire to hold jealously to their position, are really very few. There are, indeed, some who frankly admit that they do not want laymen to preach, because they look upon the pulpit as their special area of competence and they do not wish to miss any opportunity to use it, but these constitute only a small minority. The average pastor, at least in America, is a highly democratic person and deeply committed to the idea set forth in this chapter. The real difficulty lies with the laymen rather than with the clergymen. Many clergymen hate to be called "Reverend" and do everything they can to resist the tendency to set them apart. It is not they, but the ordinary laymen who, in most instances, speak of men "of the cloth," and expect religious functions to be performed by persons of a professional class. If we are to change the situation we must change the attitudes of the laymen; the clergy are, for the most part, ready for a change now. Many pastors are embarrassed by the tendency to call on them for official prayers, and wish such opportunities could be more widely spread, but the pressure of convention is so great that most pastors acquiesce rather than act so as to cause trouble.

The existence of a large body of able and sincere pastors is one of the most hopeful factors in our present situation. If we can match them with still greater numbers of concerned laymen, men who are willing to break the religious conventions of the recent past, our time may be one of genuine hope. Good pastors need have no fear, since the basic Christian pattern of organization really ennobles, rather than degrades, the work of the pastor or teacher. He is successful, not insofar as he makes men depend upon him, but rather insofar as he can help them to make their own religious lives strong. One of the chief ways of measuring the success of a professional religious worker is to note "the extent to which he increases the number and efficiency of the volunteer workers."[2] Ordinarily a man is not a good pastor unless his influence is infectious or highly multiplying. The really successful preacher will have those who have heard him clamoring for opportunities to preach. A religion that is not contagious is not genuine.

[2] John R. Mott, *Liberating the Lay Forces of Christianity* (New York: The Macmillan Company, 1932), p. 84.

Gibbon has a famous chapter on the causes of the rapid spread of Christianity in the inhospitable soil of the Roman Empire, a development he could not deny, however unsympathetic he may have been. He assigned first place to the fact that "it became the most sacred duty of a new convert to diffuse among his friends and relations the inestimable blessing which he had received."[3] John R. Mott, himself a powerful example of what the lay minister can be, has described the universal ministry of the early Church in memorable words as follows:

The disciple discussed with his teacher and fellow students the Christian truth which had laid powerful hold upon him. The slave who had fallen under the spell of the One who had come to proclaim release to captives could not refrain from pointing to the Great Deliverer. Wherever the Christian disciples scattered, the evidences multiplied of Christianity as a leaven working quietly for the conversion of one household after another. It is this commending by life and by word the reality and wonder-working of the Living Lord on the part of the rank and file of His disciples within the sphere of their daily calling that best explains the penetration of Roman society with the world conquering Gospel.[4]

This is what we seek to recover in the burst of new Christian life in our day that is known as the ministry of the laity. The major success of the Christian mission in the first century arose from the conviction of the amateur and the same can occur in the twentieth century. It has been our heresy to allow most of such forces to be dormant

[3] Edward Gibbon, *The History of the Decline and Fall of the Roman Empire* (London: Methuen and Company, 1896), Vol. II, p. 7.

[4] Mott, *op. cit.*, pp. 2, 3.

when the need has been tragic. Our heresy has been to look upon the church as a society in which a few speak and many listen. Consequently, there has arisen the strange idea that the primary Christian observance of most people is that of listening to sermons. There are many who, when they try to reform a bit, piously undertake to do some sermon listening.

Now sermons *may* be wonderful, and some actually are, but the notion that listening to human words is an especially religious act is very far from self-evident. In practice sermon listening may be a vice, because it may be a substitute for a more effective witness. John R. Mott has been especially helpful at this point by saying:

> A multitude of laymen are today in serious danger. It is positively perilous for them to hear more sermons, attend more Bible classes and open forums and read more religious and ethical works, unless accompanying it all there be afforded day by day an adequate outlet for their new-found truth.[5]

The insufficiency of sermon hearing as a religious exercise is well demonstrated in the life of James Boswell, whose newly published *London Journal* reveals that his frequent practice of listening to sermons did not prevent him from planning, at the same time, his outrageous escapades. We need to understand that the Christian witness lies not in some passive attendance, but rather in sharing the missionary effort at some point in human contact. In this case, at least, it is more blessed to give than to receive and men learn more of Christian truth by what they share than by what they hear.

[5] *Ibid.*, p. 43.

What is wrong in the accepted contemporary pattern is not the sermon, but the lay *attitude*. If thousands of men and women were to attend public worship in the mood of participation, praying for the speaker, and going with real devotional preparation, great things might result. Whether the church be liturgical or nonliturgical, the sermon may be a way in which a sensitive interpreter, knowing the people and their problems by intimate contact, reaches the deep places in individual lives and consequently helps men and women on their way. But this will not usually occur so long as the average lay member attends in the mood of the spectator. Once participation in spirit is genuine, however, the sermon can immediately become the means of bringing perplexed people to able pastors for counsel and help in a multitude of ways. Thus the greater the emphasis on lay religion the more rewarding the relationship between pastor and people.

A gesture in the direction of lay ministry is made in many churches today by the observance annually of a Layman's Sunday. Sometimes a layman gives the sermon, though more often a professional speaker does this, while laymen manage other parts of the service. This may be a start in the right direction, but it is certainly a feeble one, and it will cease to be really effective unless it is greatly enlarged. Every Sunday ought to be Layman's Sunday. A magnificent opportunity is lost in many churches at the time of the pastor's annual vacation. How little the full idea of the new reformation is grasped is shown by the almost universal practice of bringing in professional religious speakers to "fill the pulpit." What a chance is thereby missed! This is the very situation in which the more concerned members, who seldom are asked to speak, could be given their golden opportunity. They would grow under the experience and, in most instances, the congregation would feel a far greater interest. Many would rather listen to one of their fellow members than to some stranger of whom they never had heard previously.

The basic error, which we must overcome if we are to have the new life that our critical days require, is an error in the notion of what a church is. Millions seem to think of the church as an organization roughly similar to an orchestra society. Unless there were the orchestra society, the orchestra could not ordinarily be employed. The duty of members is to support the orchestra, which the city needs, and along with their support goes the privilege of attendance at concerts. But, during the performances, the society members are merely observers or auditors or both; they can sit in a relaxed way, since the responsibility lies with those on the platform.

The relevant remark is to the effect that, if Christians were to understand themselves aright, they would realize that their closer resemblance is to the *orchestra,* not to the orchestra society. In the basic Christian pattern there may be a division of labor, and there may be a conductor, but *all play.* All are performers rather than auditors or observers. A person who joins the church joins in a functioning, working group and he volunteers for a task. If this change of figure should become general in the popular Christian mentality, revolutionary results would follow.

The production of this change is the first task of those who are devoted to the cause of lay religion.

If we should take lay religion seriously, as was done in the early Christian Church, the dull picture, presented by so many contemporary churches, would be radically altered. Men and women of all professions and of all ages would gather, not to watch others perform, but to take counsel together, to witness, to pray, and to gain strength for the conduct of their individual ministries. The pastors would play a significant and creative part in this enterprise, not by performing while others watch, but by helping to stir up the ministry of the ordinary members.

As the modern Christian movement has developed, most successful pastors are overworked. They are harassed by telephone calls and they are expected to share in a multitude of community enterprises. The general theory is that they have a great deal of free time and can, accordingly, be called upon for a variety of services. In addition they are supposed to deal with many individual problems, to visit in homes and hospitals, to prepare stimulating sermons, to read widely and to manage what is really a large business enterprise. When a building is being erected and paid for the business side may assume even larger proportions.

It is easy to see that it is not possible for any individual to perform even the major tasks of the pastorate unless he has a good deal of help. The way to get this help is to use human assets hitherto unemployed in this particular way. In each church we could organize a Volunteer Corps which would produce the double benefit of relieving the hard-pressed pastor and of giving an outlet to valuable powers among the laymen.

One very important source of man power, now largely unexploited, is provided by the growing company of retired persons. If we take the idea of lay religion seriously we may be able to exploit this resource and accordingly make a big difference in the Christian cause. The present pattern which we follow in our American culture, with some minor exceptions, is that of a few men giving full time to Christian work while most other men give full time, or almost full time, to secular work, particularly to that in which success is measured by monetary gain. The secular workers are supposed to help support the committed ones in their Christian work, but to do little of it themselves. When the secular workers finally come to the age of retirement, the pattern requires that they occupy the remainder of their lives in idleness or in the vain pursuit of happiness, by means of entertainment. It is well known that the lives of many such retired men are both empty and frustrating. Above all, the social pattern we normally follow is terribly wasteful, because we fail to use what is available.

Now, the proposition is simply this: that we abolish the concept of retirement. Whatever the worldly expectation may be, Christians should be people who rule out retirement as unchristian or absurd. This does not mean that a man necessarily goes on with the same secular job until he dies, but rather that he faces life with the expectation of change. A Christian may conclude a job, but he cannot leave a cause. The late Clarence Johnson, who left the

Purina Mills to become head of the Program of Progress
of the Southern Presbyterian Church, did not retire at
fifty-seven; what he did was to change from promoting
the sale of grain to promoting the spread of the Christian
gospel. Many of the same skills were carried over from one
job to the other, but a new zest came into the man's life
because of the new purpose.

The problem of retired men is becoming an ever more
insistent one in our culture because of the new vigor of
old age which modern medicine has made possible. We
are going to have, in the near future, many strong persons
who are considerably beyond middle age, and, unless we
change our ideas, the waste will be tremendous. This is
where the Church ought to be ahead of the world.

There are countless tasks in the promotion of the Christian cause that could be done by persons who have given
large blocks of energy to other pursuits, but who finally
join a Volunteer Christian Corps. Some would need modest salaries, but many others, who have been able to acquire
a competence and do not want to end their lives in the
pursuit of triviality, would need no salary at all. One of
the ways in which men of commercial or industrial experience could be useful would be in the business management of churches. Many of our strong churches now demand so much of their pastors in business management
that these harassed men have little time or energy left for
their prophetic tasks. The way out is to find others who
are glad to volunteer their services and thus engage in a
productive lay ministry.

Important as may be the work of older persons who are

able to leave their major employment in order to engage fully in the lay ministry, there is another work which is even more important, that which can occupy the free time of men who are still regularly employed in secular tasks. The concerned layman need not wait until the ordinary age of retirement to join the Volunteer Corps. He can join it at any age, because there are so many tasks to be done that all can be used. The average pastor would be heartened beyond expression if it should become standard in a congregation for large numbers of members engaged in common pursuits to volunteer for Christian work. If the modern emphasis on the ministry of the laity catches our imagination this practice will become standard.

Nearly all who care about the Christian cause are familiar with the lifework of John R. Mott. Though always a layman, in the sense that he has never been ordained, Dr. Mott was early liberated, by generous backers, from the necessity of earning a living and has thus been free to devote his energies in whatever ways seemed most promising, regardless of economic considerations. The contagious influence of this one man, in a public career of more than sixty years, is something for which every Christian must be immensely grateful. If young men of our generation can be inspired, as the young John Mott was inspired, we can make a real difference. But how was he inspired? His interest was caught by a layman named J. E. K. Studd, who came as a cricketer from the University of Cambridge to Cornell. This man, who later became Lord Mayor of London, Dr. Mott has said, "was the means of leading me into a vital and reasonable faith in Christ."

The visiting athlete could not have dreamed how far his evangelistic effort was to spread, through John R. Mott's remarkable career, but he kindled the young man of Cornell as no professional had been able to do. The Mott career is a brilliant demonstration of what the vocation of the amateur may mean.

It is not necessary for a layman to have talents like those of Dr. Mott or those of the man who first reached him, in order to be of effective service for the Christian cause. For most laymen the chief opportunities for ministry will not appear on a world scale, but on a restricted local scale, and that is as it should be. There would be no World Council of Churches if there were not faithful local churches in countless communities, and there cannot be local churches without concerned lay men and women, who are engaged in the ministry of common life, especially in daily work and in the conduct of homes. The consideration of these common types of ministry will constitute the next two chapters.

CHAPTER III

The Ministry of Work

> Laying stress upon the importance of work has a greater
> effect than any other technique of living in the direc-
> tion of binding the individual more closely to reality.
> SIGMUND FREUD

IN THE previous chapter an argument has been presented for volunteer Christian work, both on the part
of the older persons who are free to give full time to the
church and on the part of those who, because they are
regularly employed, can give away only a margin of their
time. We are making a serious mistake, however, if, in
stressing this volunteer work, we seem to suggest that work
is not Christian work unless it is work for the churches.
Actually the witness made in regular employment may be
far more significant and productive than any service ren-
dered in free time. It is a gross error to suppose that the
Christian cause goes forward solely or chiefly on week
ends. What happens on the regular weekdays may be far
more important, so far as the Christian faith is concerned,
than what happens on Sundays. A minority ought to
leave their secular employment in order to engage in full-

time work, for the promotion of the gospel, but this is not true of most. Most men ought to stay where they are and to make their Christian witness *in* ordinary work rather than beyond it. A deeply concerned banker may be sorely tempted to leave his bank in order to give his full time to some volunteer service, but deeper reflection may show him that this would be a mistake. The investment of funds, especially for great charities, may be a task which it would be wrong for such a man to escape.

One of the heartening developments of our time has been the growing awareness, on the part of those touched by the Christian gospel, of the meaning of vocation. The idea is that God can call us to many kinds of activity and that secular work well done is a holy enterprise. We have reacted violently, and with good reason, against the medieval heresy to the effect that there are religious levels, with common work in the world appearing at the bottom. Once many believed that it was best to be one of "the religious," associated with some monastic order, that it was second best to be a secular priest, and that it was third best to be an ordinary workman. Most of us now see this conception as a monstrous distortion of Christian truth, but it is still necessary to struggle against vestiges of it. A workman, who is asked what ministry he is in, will usually reply, "I'm not a minister, I'm a carpenter." There is still much to do if we are to make the ordinary carpenter believe that he has a holy calling.

The degree to which a change is beginning to appear is shown by the success of writings and conferences on the subject of work. When Wallace Speers wrote, for the

American Magazine, an article entitled "Going to Work with God on Monday,"[1] he had no way of knowing how explosive the response would be. Letters poured in from all parts of the world, showing that the idea seemed novel, yet was, at the same time, one for which many are now ready. One of the most notable of Christian gatherings of the last few years was the first North American Lay Conference on "The Christian and His Daily Work." Three hundred twenty-five men, from the United States and Canada, met at Buffalo to learn together the religious significance of ordinary vocations. The central conviction, stated by Professor Robert L. Calhoun of Yale, on the opening day, was that "the layman's occupation is not something separate from religion, any more than hands are separate from mind and heart. Devoted work is the very flesh and bone of living religion, without which worship cannot live and grow."

In the Buffalo conference there was an effort to see the religious obligations of the farmer, the industrialist, the union laborer, the lawyer, the scientist and many more. Christian standards, it was observed, set special problems for attorneys, who must, insofar as they are Christian, be concerned with something more than the secular law. Similar problems arise for the Christian doctor; the way he takes care of the sick, regardless of ability to pay, is probably the chief way in which his ministry can be expressed.

Reports of new development in the effort to apply the

[1] Available as a reprint from The Layman's Movement, 347 Madison Avenue, New York 17, N. Y.

concept of Christian vocation come steadily from many parts of the earth. Thus we have the news from Edinburgh of the formation of a lay order, within the Church of Scotland, for the promotion of religion in industry. The new organization, known as "The Scottish Christian Industrial Order" will seek to encourage participation by Christians in trade and professional organizations and to promote understanding of the relevance of the gospel to modern industrial situations.

Though the institution of the Sabbath has been one of the most beneficent social inventions in the history of mankind, encouraging a wholesome rhythm in the week, and even making the week a meaningful idea, there are ways now in which concentration upon the one day of worship may be harmful. It is harmful whenever such concentration involves the relegation of all of the rest of the week to pagan standards of success. In an earlier agricultural economy the concentration of religious interests into one day each week was naturally the best that could be done, but, in a highly urbanized economy, it is possible that the chief witness of many must be made on the weekdays.

Consider the predicament of an old church in the heart of commercial London. Once it was close to people's homes, but it is so no longer. Practically nobody lives in the district, though several hundred thousand work there five days a week. By the end of the week they are thoroughly tired of the noise of the city so that most of those who can manage to do so naturally seek rest in rural places. It would not only be foolish to expect these people to come into the city again on Sunday; it would be wicked to try to bring them back. What, then, is the church to do? If the church is primarily a Sunday institution there is *nothing* for the church to do, but fortunately that is not the case. What such a church *can* do is to *invade the weekday*.

In one church which is located in the heart of London the leaders do not try to do much on Sunday, but they make an effective witness in the working day. Men are appointed as chaplains in industry and early weekday communion services are arranged for office workers Monday through Friday. Most of all an effort is made to help the employed persons to see the religious significance of their secular tasks. This is a heartening example of how the ongoing Christian movement can adapt itself to changing situations instead of clinging to outmoded and therefore unsuccessful forms of strategy.

The chief glory of work lies in the fact that it is really the only thing we can give that is our *own*. We do not produce our talents or the natural resources with which we work, but we do produce our *toil*. A carpenter who builds a beautiful bench cannot claim to have provided the wood or the other materials, yet he may be truly creative in the sense that, after his work has been done, there is something of beauty and of utility in the world that would not have existed, apart from his devoted labor. The result is different because he has put into it his energy, his thought and his moral stamina. We may be *stewards* of our talents, but we are *donors* of our labor.

There is no doubt that this idea, expressed by many, is one of the great ideas of the world, going back in essence even to the Hebrew Psalms,[2] but the sad truth is that the idea has not even penetrated the majority of those who toil. Most work in any modern industrialized society, far from seeming to be a thrilling adventure in unique creation, is felt to be merely *boring*. Indeed one reason why so many persons engage in gambling is that this is the only way in which life seems to them bearable. For millions of our countrymen the excitement of gambling on the horses is really the only excitement they have. John Oliver Nelson is undoubtedly reporting accurately when he says, "Even though we have more Americans these days at work than ever before—boom days of prosperity because of war-based economy—a vast proportion of them find no real challenge, no vision, no excitement in what they do to earn their living."

It is important to say that work which has no other incentive than the pay check is closer to slavery than it is to freedom. A great part of our modern tragedy consists in the fact that boredom is our chief occupational disease. It is obvious that we cannot build a good society this way, no matter how high the resultant standard of living may be, measured in technological devices. Our success will be merely superficial, and probably transitory, unless we can help the rank and file to have deeper reasons for daily toil.

There is increasing evidence that this problem cannot be solved on a merely secular basis, but we have much reason to believe that it can be solved on a basis of Christian commitment. We know that our faith, far from being a mere decoration, is something which makes a genuine

[2] Ps. 90:17.

practical difference when we find a garage mechanic or finisher of floors who envisages his daily work as the chief expression of the gospel, so far as his own life is concerned. We must have great respect for the unbelieving mechanic who tries to be scrupulously honest, but something is added to this when Christian commitment comes in. Part of what is added is the sense of joy that comes to a believer who is convinced that, humble as he is, he is a partner of the Living God, helping minutely in the work of creation. There is a world of difference between a building operation in which the workmen, however competent they may be, have their eyes on the clock, and one in which the workmen see their total task as a holy calling. We have seen buildings constructed in the latter way, even in our own time, and the resultant gains have been truly great. This is hard for those who have not experienced it to understand, but, once we see it, we cannot doubt.

The word "vocation" has been debased in the modern world by being made synonymous with "occupation," but it is one of the gains of our time that the old word is beginning to regain its original meaning of "calling." "Behold your calling, brethren," is the old text which is now achieving new significance. On the purely secular basis the term "vocation" is practically meaningless, since, unless God really is, there is no one to do the calling, but, on the Christian basis, it is a reasonable word. It still refers, in many cases, to occupation, but the conception is that each occupation can and must be conceived as a *ministry*.

The exciting idea behind the New Testament use of

"calling" is that ours is God's world, in all its parts. The way in which we grow potatoes is as much a matter of God's will as is the way in which we pray or sing. Of all precious elements in God's world, men and women are most precious, because they share something of the divine life, particularly in the capacity to be creative. Toil then becomes holy, because it is by toil that men can prove themselves creatures made in God's image. The Bible story begins with emphasis on God as *worker,* in making the world, and then stresses the creation of man in God's image. If God is the Worker, then men and women, in order to fulfill their potentialities, must be workers, too. They are sharing in creation when they develop a farm, paint a picture, build a home or polish a floor.

The most exciting part of this developing Biblical idea is that God has a purpose for each man's life. The notion that the God of all the world has a private interest in every human being who is or was or will be is a staggering notion. Many find it flatly unbelievable. They point out the size of this undertaking, in view of the millions in all the towns and villages today, but go on to say that these are only a fraction of the men and women who have lived. Since our earth is only one planet, associated with one of many suns, it is conceivable that there are countless conscious beings in other parts of the universe. How, they ask, can even God know them all and have a particular intention for each?

In answer we may freely admit that the idea is staggering, but it is relevant to reply that Jesus believed it to be true. If the idea is false there is no avoiding the conclusion that Jesus was wrong at his point of deepest faith. *Now the Christian conviction is that Jesus was not wrong.* By this we stand or fall. A Christian is one who is deeply convinced that God knows each person thoroughly, is able to have a personal relation with each and has a purpose for every life. Because God has made man free, it is possible for us to resist His love and thereby fail to fulfill His intention for us. God always knocks, but we are so made that we can refuse to answer. God makes the vocation, but we can fail to follow it, because God works by affection rather than by coercion. We can deny our vocation, either by insensitivity to God's call, so that we fail to hear, or by disloyalty after we have heard.

A great part of the vitality of early Christianity, mentioned in Chapter II, arose from this conviction of divine intention. Imagine a slave who was told that Christ died for *him*, and that there was a divine purpose for him to fulfill! Men who believe that they are servants of God are hard to stop, whatever their work in the world may be. Aquila and Priscilla, as is well known, made tents for a living, but their evangelistic vigor was so great that they are mentioned in three books of the New Testament.[3] It was modest people like these, filled with a sense of divine vocation, making their very work a ministry, who brought renewal to ancient civilization and introduced a new spirit in the midst of moral depression.

It has been difficult, in succeeding centuries, to hold the high ground which the early Christians won. The idea of vocation remained, and was often mentioned in suc-

[3] Acts 18:2, 26; Rom. 16:3; I Cor. 16:19.

ceeding generations, but it was reduced in value by being applied to a mere part of the Christian society, rather than to all members potentially. In recent generations we have frequently limited the notion of a call to what is termed a "call to the ministry," meaning by this, in essence, a call to the pastorate or to the foreign mission field. This use of the term was not wrong, but it was woefully inadequate. Now we are finding, in various parts of the Christian movement, a conscious effort to recover the earlier and more vital conception. Today, in Christian Youth Conferences, young people pledge themselves to the ministry of farming and the ministry of medicine or law, right along with those who pledge themselves to the ministry of the pastorate. This is a great gain for which we have reason to be thankful and which ought to prevail more widely than it now does.

The rebirth and wider application of the idea of vocation is a sound reason for seeing our distraught time as a time of genuine reformation. Much of the power of the Reformation of the sixteenth and seventeenth centuries arose from a rediscovery of the idea of vocation then, as men applied to common life many of the principles formerly associated with the lives of monks and nuns. Perhaps each generation needs to experience its own rediscovery of the meaning of vocation, because reformation zeal tends to dwindle.

It is a great help to get the idea straight, for that constitutes a sound beginning, but we need to be reminded that it is only a beginning; the main practical problems for each life remain. It helps to believe that God is just as much interested in the life plans of carpenters as He is in the life plans of preachers, but how do we go forward from this point? Granted that the noblest ministry is the ministry of common work, how is it to be performed? At this point many must be honestly puzzled and we ought to help one another as much as possible.

In trying to answer such a question we must understand that no simple answer is possible. Since each man's life is different from all others, no single pattern will apply to all. Indeed the ministry of work is much harder to accomplish than is the ordinary professional ministry of the ordained clergy. For the ordained men there is an accepted and well-tried way of doing things. In their careers there is a well-established and popularly known set of procedures, but for the ministry of the lawyer there are no such generally known ways. For the pastor there is the routine of calling, of the conduct of services and of personal counseling, but the garage mechanic who wishes sincerely to make his work a ministry has no accepted pattern to follow. Probably he will have to work it out for himself, by long experience of trial and error, before he feels sure that he has found the way, and even then he will not be wholly satisfied.

In spite of the difficulty, there are undoubtedly a few general ideas than can be applied to all kinds of work and we ought to try to learn what they are. One idea is that almost every job in the world is a job in which there are many contacts with other human beings. The work of some is primarily with persons, while the work of others is primarily with things, but nearly all deal with other persons at some point in each day. Many jobs are terribly routine, so that boredom is easy, but nearly always there are fellow workers on the production line. The ways in which these people are greeted and the ways in which conversation goes on at lunch time may seem unimportant, but, in the long run, this is how we convince one another of our sincerity in caring. The friendships started in this way may give opportunity, on other occasions, of conversation at deeper levels when severe crises are encountered. Such crises come to all, but we have to earn the right in advance if we are to be useful to our fellows at such times.

The most serious question about these contacts with other persons, in the course of employment, is the question of our attitude toward each person. Do I see my boss merely as employer or do I realize that he, too, is one for whom God has an intention? As a merchant do I see men and women merely as *customers* or primarily as *persons* who incidentally are my customers? If I am an employer of others, do I see each worker as a person in his own right? The temptation is to see him as merely a cog in my machine. Here it is the Christian conviction that provides a genuine alternative to our present industrial struggle for power. There would still be industrial and commercial problems if all concerned were deeply committed Christians, because problems involving great numbers are not simple, but there are no problems that cannot be solved by the kind of good will just described.

The ordinary worker who seeks to make his work a ministry can make great strides in this direction by the introduction of prayer and meditation into his work.

Much as we may need to pray when we are in church, we often need to pray far more when we are engaged in difficult mental or manual tasks. Why should not a Christian businessman pray on every occasion when he faces a difficult decision, especially when there may be some personal clash? Why should not every teacher pray for strength as he walks through the hall of the school to face a class? Such a person need not parade his piety at all, for prayer can be genuine without any change in external posture. It may be fair to say that a job about which a Christian cannot pray is not the right job and is therefore outside his true vocation.

The problem of the routine task, which seems to be a necessary element in our industrial economy, is one which we must never evade or minimize. If, however, a man can honestly feel that the final product, of which his routine contribution is a part, is something good or useful for mankind, there is a deep sense in which his toil is glorified. It is a shame that some tasks are dull, but it is important to realize that nearly all tasks are dull at some point or other. The life of the production line worker is not wholly enviable, but it can be brought into the context of Christian experience providing (a) the human contacts are fully exploited, (b) the work contributes to a good end and (c) the free time, outside the factory, is creatively employed.

We must not forget, whenever we discuss, as we so often do, the plight of the modern factory worker, that there are men and women who are *not* bored by factory work. There are some who enjoy it and who look forward to each day. They are the workers who find interest in the human contacts or who use their time on the job to think creatively of better ways of doing and living. Each person who succeeds in this way is helping to demonstrate that the situation is not nearly as hopeless as we have conventionally supposed.

A harder question than that of the dull but honest job is posed by the job that is parasitical or harmful. It is easy to say that *all* jobs may become scenes of lay ministry, but to say so is to engage in overstatement. There are some ways of earning that are not really open to concerned Christian men, because Christian men cannot perform them with self-respect. This is conspicuously true of those who engage in the far-flung business of gambling. Or what shall we say of the vicious modern occupation of dope peddling, victimizing the young?

Nearly all thoughtful people will reject these obviously harmful occupations and grant that they cannot become vocations, but what of tasks which are merely trivial? How must a man feel, in the light of serious human needs, if he gives the major energies of his life to the production and dissemination of perfume for men? What is the moral defense of those who publish confession magazines and of those who write the stories for these magazines, often under names which hide their identity? Perhaps it is right to say that we can never, in the light of Christian convictions, engage in trivial occupations when this involves a *waste* of powers that could be used in better ways.

Waste is the real tragedy of countless lives. It is seldom tragic to die, but it is extremely tragic to go on living in meaningless ways when meaningful ways are possible.

It is a shameful thing for a healthy person to devote the majority of his time to keeping his own body alive and his own affairs in order, with no considerable margin left over for service to those who cannot sufficiently help themselves; it is always shameful to be primarily a problem when we might be part of the answer; it is always shameful to be a parasite when it is possible to be a producer. John Oliver Nelson, in his widely quoted address before the Centennial meeting of the Young Men's Christian Association at Cleveland, clarified many minds by the following dictum: "Almighty God doesn't call any man or woman to a trivial or unimportant life work. If you can't see your job as being somehow vital and meaningful to mankind, change it or get out of it."[4] These are true words. God's purpose is frustrated every time a human being works at something trivial or harmful.

There is a true contemporary story, most revealing at this point, of an advertising man in a great American city whose special assignment was the promotion of a certain whiskey. He was a skilled man in his profession and knew how to make the product appealing to prospective customers. As a result of his ability and success he was well paid and had built up for his suburban home a high standard of living expense. Many, in the light of secular standards, would consider such a man an outstanding success. But the day came when the man began to lose respect for himself. He was not only convinced that his advertising was harmful; he was convinced also that it was insincere.

[4] *Every Occupation a Christian Calling* (New York: Association Press, 1951), p. 9.

He labored mightily to convince readers and hearers that his client's whiskey was better than others of its type, when he felt sure in his own heart that the whole claim was a lie. Consequently, he went home one day and announced that he was through and, to the amazement of neighbors and friends, began to engage in productive work that brought in only a fraction of the income of his former position. He did all this because the idea of Christian vocation had gone deeply into his life.

Such a story is wonderfully heartening, but the sad truth is that there are thousands, in roughly similar predicaments, who never have the courage to make the break. Often they believe sincerely that the break is impossible. They have built up so many financial responsibilities in connection with their families that they never consider themselves free to change, so they go on all their lives in galling bondage, with their self-respect becoming less and less with each succeeding year. It would not be right to urge people to be changeable in their work, because most jobs have more possibilities than is usually realized and the temptation to see greener grass on the other side of the fence is a common one. Some of those who change are merely escaping from a challenging situation and this action must never be encouraged, but the fact remains that many *ought to change*. There is no great likelihood that people will always get into the right work the first time they try. To go on with a job for which one is unfitted and which he cannot respect is not courageous, but merely mulish.

For the Christian the task of change is made easier by

the conviction that really useful work, so far as a Christian
is concerned, can never be judged by worldly standards
of higher and lower. It is part of our secular snobbery to
feel that some work is respectable while other work lowers
the social standing of a family. Frequently a student is a
bit ashamed to admit to his professor that his father is a
truck driver. It would sound so much better if he were
a doctor. But, as far as the Christian community is concerned, this snobbishness must be rejected wholly. We
must believe again in the deep democracy of work. If
truck driving is needed to feed and clothe and house our
people, then truck driving is noble and can be a holy
calling. Providing the work is beneficent, the understanding Christian will never apologize for it.

There is no doubt that money can be a boon to mankind
when rightly used, but the time soon comes when a person
who is moved primarily by the Christian idea of vocation
cannot be satisfied with the sole incentive of making
money. There are heartening stories of contemporary
Christian laymen who, even in middle life, with great
financial rewards just ahead, have changed jobs, not because the original job was trivial or evil in its consequences,
but because the man became convinced that he had powers
which the original job did not demand or develop. It is a
shame to go down to the grave with some outstanding
talent undeveloped, merely because there has never been
a job to draw it out or the will to bring it forth with
arduous self-discipline.

Just as the Christian cannot be satisfied to work for
money, he likewise cannot be satisfied with mere technical

skill. It is easy to see that technical skill can be used for a great variety of ends, some of them harmful rather than helpful to the human race. It is sobering to realize that the men engaged in cancer research, to which we owe so much and to whom we shall owe more, *could* use their knowledge and skill to *spread* cancer rather than to decrease it. Of course they do not, but the reasons for not doing so are not technological reasons. All of them work on the basis of an unstated premise, which is not the less significant for being unstated, the premise that it is better to minister than to be ministered unto. What makes cancer research into a boon, instead of a possible curse, is the addition to skill of the concept of vocation. The task is made holy by its purpose and by its human consequences.

It is hard to think of any job in which the moral element is lacking. The skill of the dentist is wholly irrelevant, if he is unprincipled and irresponsible. There is little in that case, to keep him from withdrawing teeth unnecessarily, because the patient is usually in a helpless situation. It is easy to see the harm that can be done by an unprincipled lawyer. Indeed, such a man is far more dangerous if he is skilled than if he is not skilled. We are accustomed to this idea of moral responsibility in what we call the professions, but something of the kind is a factor in more common jobs. The house painter can cheat on his materials, the well-paid workman can squander his time. Part of our present inflation in costs, which may ultimately be so damaging to our society that collapse follows, arises from such moral causes.

The sincere application of the principle of work as a

ministry would be an antidote to most of these troubles. Part of what we need in economic order is a revival of common honesty. It is conceivable that men of our time might come to take pride in meticulous care in the keeping of promises and strictness with themselves in matters of integrity. There have been periods like that before and they could come again, but they will not come of themselves. We are making a start in this direction when we give the widest possible dissemination to the idea that no amount of piety on Sunday will take the place of integrity on Wednesday. Unless we can go to work with God on Monday we are not likely, in the long run, to have any effective worship of God on Sunday, and if we do engage in the latter, it becomes a sham.

Having said this, we must, in order to tell the truth, go on to say that there must be in every good life, not only honest toil, but also respite from such toil. The person who always works is missing the good life as truly as does the person who never works. The Jewish institution of the Sabbath was a social invention of the first magnitude, which can contribute to all mankind, but which modern man has largely lost. The unfortunate fact is that, in our Western civilization, the day of alleged rest has become only another day of intense activity. It is good to be active, but there must come regularly in every life a "wise passiveness in which the soul lies open to whatever forces from any direction may touch it."[5] We cannot recover the true glory of work unless we likewise recover the glory of rest.

[5] Lewis Mumford, *The Conduct of Life* (New York: Harcourt, Brace and Company, 1951), p. 259.

Work is by its very nature hard; that is why it is not the same as self-indulgent relaxation. There is not much hope for us if we always want everything the easy way. We ought to expect difficult situations in every worth-while job and to take satisfaction in the hardness. The older we grow the more we realize that very few lives are easy. If there are no other problems, there are those of misunderstanding and envy and jealousy. Such is nearly always part of the price which men and women must pay if they try to achieve excellence in any field. We may as well know, before we start, that mediocrity resents excellence and attacks it accordingly. If a man develops his powers effectively he is likely to be thought overconfident or proud; if he becomes a leader in industrial or professional life, many will seek to protect their own comparative failure by spreading the word that he is self-seeking; if he accepts his political responsibilities and shows any signs of succeeding, he will be the target for thousands.

We ought to change this all that we can, but we know that it is a long-time task, of enormous difficulty. Meanwhile, there are Christian resources on which men could draw in such circumstances, the best resource being the conviction of the existence of God's plan. A man who feels, with reasonable certainty, that he is following something of God's intention for his own life can bear great hardships without frustration and likewise without self-pity. Wonder comes into any life in which it is seriously proposed to become to the Living God what a man's own hand is to a man. Reinold von Thadden, the eminent lawyer and lay leader of Germany, has told various American audiences of how this basic conviction upheld him in the cruelty of prison camps immediately after the end of the war, but his is only one illustration out of many that could be given. The sense of God's intention is a sense that makes a difference in a man's life and has made weak men bold.

An essential element in all faith is the factor of risk. True faith is never unwillingness to face uncomfortable facts, but is always a willingness to face boldly the consequences of a position which is taken on principle. We ought to consider very seriously what is to be learned from the immense and growing vogue of gambling, which has even invaded the field of intercollegiate athletics. It is widely recognized that this vogue of gambling is a symptom of the dullness of ordinary life and particularly of daily work.

We cannot deal intelligently or adequately with this problem by giving good advice or telling how evil gambling is. We cannot deal with it unless we help to provide in men's lives excitement and risk so genuine that the pseudo-risk of petty gambling will no longer seem attractive. Where, except in the concept of a double vocation, can this be provided? A man who sees his daily work as a way in which his loyalty to the Christian cause can be demonstrated may face abundant risk in his life. Not many will do anything as dramatic as the action of the advertising man who left his lucrative position when he became convinced of the insincerity of his work, but many can exhibit more modest versions of the same pattern. It ought to be standard, for example, for a Christian to accept a lower paid position rather than a higher paid one, providing the lower paid one meets his minimum needs and permits a far wider use of his creative powers. This is essential to all commitment and ought to be taken for granted in Christian circles. But there are other risks which are not primarily financial. A Christian must be willing to take the less glamorous or less honored position if his sense of divine intention leads him, by that means, to a way of greater service. Furthermore, the following of this intention will often bring genuine unpopularity, especially when a man is convinced that he must stand against accepted standards of moral action.

Since the method of queries, designed to facilitate individual searching of heart, is a well-tested one, any worker may profitably ask him seriously the following questions:

1. Am I involved currently, either in my work or out of it, in a sense of risk? Does the pursuit of my vocation take me, at any point, beyond what is safe, comfortable, accepted or popular?

2. Do I, both in my working hours or outside, find some means of witnessing to my faith? Do I, without any ostentation, let those who work near me understand the basic motivation of my life?

3. Am I, at some point, truly creative? Do I explore the opportunities for growth and novelty inherent in my situation and make full use of them or am I entrapped in accepted stereotypes of procedure?

4. Am I diligent to *learn*, reaching out to enlarge my knowledge and seeking to grow every day, so that

my sights are really kept high? Or am I satisfied with a modicum of effectiveness, without the full use of all of my powers?

5. Am I identified with a dedicated group, including those whose daily work is widely different from my own? Do I experience the power that is released by a small, intimate group of persons united, not by their training, but by their common Christian commitment?

There are probably many more questions which we should ask ourselves and each thoughtful reader will add to the list just given, but if we should ask ourselves these five questions, we should find many subtle changes beginning to occur. All of this reinforces the idea, mentioned earlier, that the ministry of work is really something which each person must figure out for himself, since there are no stereotypes to follow. Each man, whatever his toil, must use his own imagination and steady prayer to try to learn what the details of his daily ministry ought to be. It is essentially a lonely undertaking, but the lonely task is made easier by the recognition that others have made the same attempt for themselves and that there are many who care.

CHAPTER IV

The Recovery of Family Life

Not for a single day did they cease to teach and preach
the gospel of Jesus the Christ, in the temple and at home.
ACTS 5:42 (Moffatt)

IMPORTANT as daily work may be, in the experience
of the ordinary human being, the life of his family
is far more important. His pride and his ambition may be
involved in his professional advancement, but far more
than pride and ambition are involved in his relationship
to his *home*. Most people, when they earn money, need
the money not as individuals, but as breadwinners for
several others, including the young and helpless. Accordingly, all the deeper emotions are involved in the effort
to support and maintain family life.

Not only is the average home a center of affections, as
a place of outside work seldom is; the home is also the
place of work for nearly half the human race. Most women,
and some men, make the home the scene of their professional existence, as it is the major scene of their emotional
existence. Thus our chapters appear in an ascending order,
so far as the lay ministry is concerned. The ministry of

80

family life includes much of the ministry of work, yet transcends it.

There is a more continuous opportunity for an effective Christian ministry in the home than anywhere else in the world. What goes on in churches is highly important, but it is always in some degree abstract, in that most of what is said to one another is out of its immediate practical context. We talk, in church, about moral values, but we talk of them in separation from the situations in which most problems arise. In a home, however, when parents instruct their children or engage in family conferences and worship, the ministry of word and deed is in the closest contact with the practical problems. The situations of selfishness and of lack of concern for others are handled directly and *in context*. Accordingly such ministry, even though the congregation is tiny, is in close touch with reality.

Another important difference between the ministry of the home and the ministry of the church lies in the fact that home ministry is always as much a matter of demonstration as of mere advice or admonition. Away from home, there is little check upon our consistency of living, but within the bosom of the family any inconsistency between word and deed is glaringly obvious. The mood of the parent who rebukes anger is noted carefully by the child and judged accordingly. No one in his right mind will ever say that we should avoid vocal teaching, but it is nevertheless true that the best teaching is that of daily demonstration. The noblest aspect of the ministry of the home lies in the degree to which preaching and practice may be mutual supports to each other, so that the home becomes more a laboratory than an auditorium.

No matter how much a man may be concerned with his work in the world, he cannot normally *care* about it as much as he cares about his family. This is because we have, in the life of the family, a bigger stake than most of us can ever have in our employment. We can change business associates, if we need to, and we can leave a poor job for a better one, but we cannot change *sons*. If we lose the struggle in our occupational interests, we can try again, but if we lose with our children our loss is terribly and frighteningly *final*. A man who cares more for his work than he cares for his family is generally accounted abnormal or perverse and justifiably so. He is one who has not succeeded in getting his values straight; he fails to recognize what the true priorities are.

We may truly say, then, that just as the lay ministry finds a fuller expression in ordinary daily work than it does in church, so it finds a fuller expression in the family than in employment, and perhaps more in the family than anywhere else in our world. If our religion does not lift the level of our family life it is not likely to be sincere or really effective at any other point. What occurs at the altar is insignificant unless what occurs there is supported by what occurs in the kitchen. The sermons by which Christian men and women may be rightly judged are the silent sermons of co-operative affection.

Many parts of our civilization are in danger of widespread decay, but no single danger is more serious than that of the decay of family life. It is no accident that the two systems which have, in our century, most challenged the free way of life, have both undermined the family. An earlier part of Bolshevik doctrine was the virtual abolition of the family, giving over to the state the chief care of the children, making divorce completely easy, and encouraging both partners in a marriage to seek employment in an industrialized economy. Essential to this was the masculinization of women and the lessening of the sacredness of the marriage tie. If the mother's chief function, outside of industry or agriculture, is merely the biological one of child-bearing, it is obvious that the home is an anachronistic institution which might as well be eliminated from an efficient social order. In Russia the earlier extreme, in this elimination of the family unit, has now given place to a more moderate view, but in China, according to recent reports, the effort to undermine the family is being carried on vigorously. It must be a severe shock to a people who have long revered the family unit to be told that the relationship to the mother is merely the biological one and that the child has no responsibility to the parents, but there is much evidence that this doctrine is now being assiduously taught. In this the group of men who began their training in Moscow, more than twenty years ago, and have now been so successful in the assumption of power, may be very astute. It may be that the change in regard to the family is more far reaching than is land reform or any other economic program of revolution.

The Nazi way of undermining the family was by the emphasis on loyalty to the state, as superseding loyalty to the family. Children were encouraged to inform against their parents, thus demonstrating the notion that love for the state far outweighed family affection. Organized youth movements are essential to all totalitarian regimes, partly because, by these devices, most of the waking hours are spent outside the home.

Our dangers to family life are not identical with those in totalitarian societies, but nevertheless real. The causes are different but, unless we can change the fashion of thinking, the end results will be strikingly similar. Though there has not been any antifamily teaching openly advocated and though we still pay lip service to the sacredness of the home, the decay proceeds. In the United States the rate of increase of divorce is greater than is the rate of increase of population, while in Great Britain, one marriage out of six ends in failure. Our latest American census shows that the situation is even worse than the official divorce figures indicate, because more than a million legally married persons are living separately without divorce. Furthermore, it is well known that many supposed homes, where people have the same official residence, are really not homes at all, because there is no unity in them.

Our standard explanation of the failure of the modern home, in the life of the West, is basically economic. With progressive inflation, and with the high standard of technological living, which mass advertising stimulates, more and more members of the family seek employment. Often a mother starts to earn because she wants to buy a televison set or some other new device, which social standing in her particular community requires. She finds that she likes work in a public place, with the lunchroom conversation or other human contacts, so she continues her outside work even though it means that her children are without care most of the day and have the added burden of two nervously tired parents when they finally come home.

The shame of many a supposed home today is that it is largely a place where people sleep part of the night, but not really a scene of uniting experiences of all members, older and younger. Common meals become more and more infrequent while unhurried family conferences are out of the question. It is futile to talk to people about grace at meals if they do not even have the meals. A couple who have to do all the housework late at night, after tiring and nervously demanding hours in the business of the day, are not prepared for family worship or even family affection. Countless supposed homes become places of bickering and of constant bitterness when the members do finally assemble. What could be the most wonderful of human associations thus becomes one of the worst.

Important as the economic factors may be in the decay of family life, they are not the most basic ones. Far more basic are the moral factors, influenced in turn by ideological considerations. What is so damaging is not the mere fact that men and women desert their family duties, but rather that millions subscribe to the doctrine of wanton self-expression. In all areas we hear people say, "This is the free world; I propose to live my own life as I please and nobody can stop me." This doctrine begins by sounding like freedom and ends as moral destruction. The men who engage in private gain at public expense are following precisely this program. Their freedom includes freedom to take bribes and they propose to do whatever they like, regardless of the consequences to others. It is not only the working mother, leaving her children at loose ends, who demonstrates this philosophy; it is equally demonstrated by the husband who, in the evening, habitually goes out with his cronies and by the socially acceptable woman who spends so much time at the bridge club or supposed social service that she neglects the one place where her influence might count most. The children of the successful men and women of the world are sometimes among the most unfortunate, in that they are denied the intimate companionship of father and mother. Men of the world, who understand this danger, are wise if they plan their lives so that there are some periods in each year when their children have a right to feel that they can enjoy their full and unhurried companionship.

Though we do not have the communist ideology to encourage the breakup of the home, we do have, in our ordinary Western life, a host of influences that are continually taking, not only the parents, but also the children away from the home circle. The life of the school becomes almost totalitarian, so far as the time of many modern children is concerned, and, when vacation comes, a host of public services are organized so that there is nearly always a *reason* why the child must go somewhere. Meals are hurriedly eaten while other children wait at the door to go to the next appointment. We know, of course, that many of these public services are good, but our danger lies in the fact that they are too numerous and too demanding. As in the totalitarian youth movements, the life of the home becomes dull and unimportant by contrast. A home ceases to be a home when most of the members are always about to leave it.

There is no possibility of developing a satisfactory social philosophy for our time or an adequate conception of the lay ministry unless we deal carefully and intelligently with the problem of woman's role in the modern world. This discussion occurs naturally in a consideration of family life because family life has been, for so many generations, the chief area in which women have made their influence felt. Thus far we have considered family life as the joint responsibility of fathers and mothers, and this it must always be, if we are to have a healthy society, but such joint responsibility does not, in any way, involve the further notion that the responsibilities of men and women are equal in this regard. Significant as the father's contribution to the moral and spiritual development of his children may be, the mother's contribution is normally, and ought to be, far *more* significant.

It is no accident that women have become the central persons in home life as men have not. For one thing, women bear children and men do not. The mere facts of pregnancy and of nursing are themselves facts that make an enormous practical difference. The Russians, when they tried to make the feminine relationship to the family identical with the masculine one, were going against this difference.

Our present ideological situation is a confused one, because, though most women have long ago revolted violently against the *Hausfrau* idea of woman's sole place being in the home, they have also begun to see that the feminist doctrine, which has largely replaced the older one, is also unsatisfactory. The antithesis is not really a significant improvement upon the thesis, but millions do not know where to turn next. Many feel that they must seek a new third way, but they need much guidance if they are to find it and to demonstrate it. It is in this search that the ministry of the Christian faith to the family may be most effective.

A great part of our trouble is that we have not helped mothers to see and to understand the glory of their central occupation. Most of our talk has been about the humdrum character of home duties, and we have said little about the need of intellectual or moral powers. We make the mistake, in our public speeches and in our writings, of glamorizing public service in the world. The young mother, hearing this kind of appeal, is moved as much as anyone else, but what can she do? She cannot rush off to do medical work with Schweitzer in Africa, because Johnny and Susie could not live a day without attentive care. People are urged to get into political action and the women who do so are honored in the magazines, but what time has the over-worked young mother for such public service?

Not only the life of men, but also the life of single women, with professional advancement and public contact, seems very attractive to many a young mother, struggling to keep the children quiet while she waits for her husband to come home to dinner. Other jobs appear to have both glamour and prestige, but hers seems to her to have *none*. It does not appear to be a task which requires any special professional competence or training, as law and medicine do, and it is not a job which normally brings either public honor or monetary reward. The chief reason why the women are conspicuously fewer than men in the listings of *Who's Who* is that excellence in the vocation, which is the vocation of the great majority of women, is not a recognized basis of inclusion. There are no doubt good reasons why this is so, but this does not keep ambitious or brilliant women from noting the *fact*.

It is hard for individual women to honor their wedded vocation of homemaking because, for the most part, the *world* does not seem to honor it. Of course we have an annual Mother's Day, but this observance is largely given over either to sentimentality or to commercialism. We know how little the tasks of motherhood are honored when we realize that few colleges take seriously the idea that young women can be prepared for such tasks with an intellectual discipline comparable to that expected in the learned professions. It is assumed that a person needs a rigorous preparation in order to be a successful architect, but the guidance of human lives is apparently thought to be on a different intellectual level.

How can we blame an ambitious and able young woman who finds herself caught in this situation? She desires an interesting life and glamour and prestige, as much as anyone else, and she determines to find a way. The unfortunate element is not her desire to find a way, but rather the fact that the way she often takes is so damaging to what is most precious both to her and to our total society.

The most obvious way of escape from her predicament is that of public employment, a way which is now supported even by some who are supposed to be experts in this field of thought.

There has appeared recently an article, sponsored by the Associated Press, in which a man who is the head of the Division of the Home and Family of a fashionable college for women reports, with commendation, the way in which the girls in his institution are "kicking over traditions to keep up with changing times and conditions." The modernism of these girls turns out to be the decision to engage in outside work after graduation, even though they are married. The professor says that only the stubbornness of men is hindering this beneficent change in the family pattern. Women must now be partners in breadwinning as well as breadmaking, says the professor, who maintains that this is the way the world is headed.

It is possible that the professor is correct in his prediction of the way in which the world is headed, but his assumption that this movement is a good one is far from self-evident. Those who uphold a pattern of living in which both husband and wife earn do not tell us what will happen to the little children during the earning hours of both. Will they be left to shift for themselves? That has been tried, and some of our worst human problems have arisen accordingly. Will the children be turned over to hired help? If so, the economic gain presented as an argument for double earning is largely canceled, while the moral and spiritual losses may be tragic. Since there is no known substitute for *mother love* the parent who believes that the moral care can be better handled by a servant is strangely lacking in self-confidence.

No doubt many of the supposed "moderns" who advocate double earning think that the problem of the children can be solved by the use of nursery schools. But the problem cannot be solved so simply. There is a superficial attractiveness about a situation in which, as in the early Leninist philosophy, each task is done by an expert. Thus the father and mother do the tasks in industry or commerce in which they became individually expert, while the children are cared for by *child* experts. Such a situation is, of course, the logical result of a society in which the principle of specialization is unchallenged, but this is a principle of which we ought to be intelligently critical. A home is a place in which the principle of specialization is consciously and deliberately challenged in favor of a higher principle, the principle of *wholeness*. Mere specialization, though it may make for efficiency, leads to the dehumanization which marks every production line. A home, by contrast to a factory, is far more similar to an organism, with all participants sharing responsibility for the total undertaking. There may be a loss in efficiency but it is more than counterbalanced by the human gain.

The production line ideal is demonstrated in the life of the child who is passed along from one specialist to another, but he is not made enviable thereby. As the late Ray Lyman Wilbur used to say, when bright young people advocated the total training of children outside the home, as a modern advance, "Children in orphanages are not conspicuously more fortunate than children in homes."

Instead of increasing the tendency to specialization, we ought to resist this tendency at many points. Since the good life comes, in such large measure, from the sense of wholeness, we ought to try to reverse the process, stimulated by the educational doctrine of the recent past, of turning over nearly all of the historic functions of the home to the school. It is not obviously true that the teacher is a better moral guide than is the parent. Lewis Mumford, in his notable work, *The Conduct of Life,* has issued a timely warning against the tendency to leave every aspect of our lives to the care of supposed experts. He says:

With rising national incomes, homes must become more generous in space to give full play to family life; social measures must be taken to help families of four or five children from being undue economic burdens to those who choose to have them; more of the functions, that have slid into the province of the school, must go back to the home, once the domestic environment of house and neighborhood is designed deliberately for the play and education of children under the tutelage of their parents.[1]

The pattern of life which includes full earning on the part of both parents, with consignment of children to the school or other public institution for most of the time, would mean, if generally adopted, the virtual destruction of the home. There would still be houses, and they might be elaborately equipped with electrical devices purchased by the extra earning of the mother, but the real center would be shifted to factory, to office and to school. The meaningful experiences would occur *chiefly* in the public

[1] *Ibid.,* pp. 283-84.

institutions rather than in the private one. As so often happens in a decaying civilization, the façade would remain, but the reality would be gone. Indeed this is what we already find in many alleged homes and the result is not attractive.

How can we find sufficient motivation and moral power to stop the decay of family life and to reverse the process that has set in? We need something stronger than the motives provided by economic considerations, partly because the more wholesome arrangement will often involve relative economic hardship and severe limitation on spending. We cannot rely and ought not to rely on any appeal to tradition, because we know that tradition can be wrong and sometimes ought to change. We cannot depend upon secular thought because the most popular secular thought tends to encourage the process of decay which we have described. The power of renewal that is needed may, however, come from the Christian faith. A great part of lay religion in our time must concern itself with the application of Christian principles to the recovery of the home.

The Christian faith looks upon the home, not as a temporary, but as a permanent institution, because it contributes supremely to ultimate values. So high does it stand in the Christian scale of values that even our relationship to God is understood in family terms. That is what the fatherhood of God means. There is a sense in which the idea of the family ought to affect the relationships of all persons to all other persons and that is what we mean when we pray, "*Our* Father." The home is the point in our culture at which there is more chance, than is found anywhere else, of demonstrating the Christian pattern in practice. Long before the Marxist ideology gave lip service to the formula, the notion of "from each according to ability and to each according to need" was understood as central to the gospel. In the teaching of Jesus, emphasis is laid on the action of giving *all* that there is to give, as in the case of the poor widow, while the prodigal son receives what he needs, regardless of his productive merit.

The application of this bold ideal is not possible at most points in our culture. We cannot do it wholly in business or in government or in education, though approximations sometimes appear in all three fields. Those industrial firms which give family allowances, depending upon the number of small children and regardless of the father's earning power, are taking a long step in this Christian direction. In many enterprises married men are better paid than are single people for similar work, and for this we should be glad. But family life differs in kind from industrial and political enterprises in that, on the domestic scene, the pattern described can be applied *fully*. There are millions of homes in which it is already true that the helpless members of the family actually receive more from the total family income than does the breadwinner or the mother. The child is not asked to wait for a pair of shoes until he has earned what the shoes cost, while the father toils when he knows that his own upkeep will amount to no more than a small fraction of his total earnings.

The family is the only institution in our world where the Kingdom of God can actually begin. This is not to paint a rosy or sentimental picture of what family life actually is. Of course, there are tensions and sometimes the strain seems so unbearable that the whole experiment ends in failure. Husbands and wives sometimes turn against each other with vindictive hatred and the same is true of parents and children, but, in an enormous number of cases, the presence of strain does not exclude a continuing and redemptive love. There are many families in which the members can truly report that, though life has been far from easy, never once has there been a real break in affection and never once has there been a struggle for power, such as most societies outside the home, including religious ones, so often exhibit. We know that homes are places where it is possible for love to be supreme and we do not know any others.

What we need, in the Christian ministry of family life, is some definite guiding lines, so that we may develop a consistent and powerful philosophy of our vocation, sufficient to resist the temptations which, when not resisted, lead to decay. *Four* of these are especially relevant.

The first guiding line is the idea of each home as a religious institution. One of the chief dangers of our secular civilization is the growing idea that marriage is merely a matter of a convenient or possibly a temporary contract. It is essential to the entire Jewish-Christian philosophy that marriage as a mere contract is only pseudo-marriage. The central act is really an act of commitment, brilliantly and vividly illustrated by the usual marriage vows in the extent to which they are unconditional. A man and a woman undertake a common destiny, not so long as both are attractive or the money holds out, but "for better, for worse; for richer, for poorer; in sickness and in health." We have what are called secular marriages, before justices of the peace, but even these, however drab the surroundings, often take on a religious significance. This is because the undertaking is *inherently* sacred.

Since commitment is central, the chief mood of major family decisions ought to be one of simple reverence. The home is a religious institution as truly as is the church or synagogue, a fact which many Jewish families have understood better than have Christian families, but the idea belongs to both religions. Herein lies the importance of family religious experience, if it be nothing more than the steady practice of grace before meat. Reliable figures are not available on this subject, but most evidence seems to indicate that the majority of contemporary families now fail to have even a perfunctory prayer or silent thanksgiving at the family table. This failure may turn out to be more important in our culture than is ordinarily realized, because it is by such habitual practices that the unconscious influence in most lives comes to be effective. A home in which there is never shared prayer is a building without a center of reference.

The essentially religious character of the home, setting it apart from industry or business, can be accentuated in many ways if the parents have imagination. Thus great moments, such as the birth of a new baby or the death of a beloved grandparent, can be faced by the household in the mood of worship. Experiences like this sink more deeply into young lives than we realize. The notion that such family experiences must be stilted or oppressive is a mere superstition. Prayer can come to be as natural as breathing and can be a joy to all concerned.

There are, of course, times of strain in every home because we are always dealing with human beings and neither angels nor automatons. We cannot expect all elimination of strain, but we *can* expect a devout way of meeting it. Many are willing to testify to the power of prayer in such situations. What might the results be if families which face serious discord should habitually meet the dangers, not merely with argument, but with genuine prayer? Such prayer might often be silent and involve a long period of waiting. In any case it would be far more than the mere repetition of conventional words, but, whatever the form, we may be sure that it would make a difference. Many report that it *does* make a difference, not in avoiding all troubling of the waters, but in showing a loving way of *navigating* the troubled waters.

A second guiding line is the frank acceptance of family life as a holy calling. The most humdrum task is raised and glorified if it is understood as a ministry to which God has called us. We know how desperately modern woman needs a heightened sense of the dignity of her work, if she is to be able to repel the temptations to escape responsibility, but this is precisely what the Christian conception provides.

A secular society is based largely on the motivation inherent in worldly rewards and honors. Persons in secular tasks of almost every kind are engaged in sharp competition with one another for advancement and recognition.

If the foreman in the factory is sufficiently able, he may be advanced to management; if the bank clerk succeeds, he may become a vice president; if the scholar succeeds, he may receive an honorary degree. In the nature of the case this competition for recognition is impossible for most married women. Indeed, they are not competing at all. We make a foolish little gesture by announcing a "Mother of the Year," but no person takes this seriously because the competition has not been genuine.

It is significant that most of the mothers of the race who *have* found worldly distinction have had to find it in extracurricular ways. They may compete for offices in clubs, but these ordinarily have nothing to do with the woman's vocation of making a center for the production of better people. Some have striven especially hard for the extracurricular honors, just *because* these are not possible in the main enterprise.

From the secular point of view the noncompetitive home situation leaves mothers, as such, out of the running, but the Christian point of view brings an utterly new light to the problem. It is the teaching of Christ that we ought *not* to seek honors, that the pagan way of distinction is to be renounced. Jesus told his followers not to be called "Rabbi" and to call no man "Father" obviously referring to a public and nondomestic title. We have disobeyed him outrageously in the church which bears his name, but it may be that the home is the one place where we *can* apply the principle. The home is inherently more Christian than any other human institution, because it transvaluates all values, by renouncing competition. We have a bit of this in other areas, as in the experience of the true scholar who does not care whether he is given a decoration or not, but in the home we can go the whole way.

If mothers could be made to understand this they would see, as few now see it, the importance of their primary role. What they can do is to substitute the concept of vocation or ministry for the concept of worldly distinction and extraneous reward.

If a woman can come to see her work in the guidance of a home as a ministry, a way in which she can fulfill the intention of God for her, she may be able to glorify her life *in her own eyes* and that is what is needed first. Motherhood is not merely a biological phenomenon; it is not merely dull domestic work; it is not merely a job; it is a holy calling. "Behold your calling" is the heartening admonition to the tired mother, who envies her husband his interesting public work, as it is to the factory worker who envies the lot of the white collar worker.

Motherhood or wifehood is a calling because it enables the person called to conduct a crucial laboratory experiment in the building of the Kingdom of God. The queen of a home stands at the point where the new world is being made—the world that needs many things, but most of all needs better people. To prepare for the ministry of home life requires as great a discipline as is required by any profession. If any one doubts this, let him consider the delicate decisions which a guide of children must make every day, many of them involving genuine dilemmas. It often seems that God should have endowed parents more adequately with brains. It is particularly inept to ask a girl whether she is going into motherhood or into a career, because the very question implies the suppressed premise that motherhood is itself *not* a career. Of course it is a career, but for a Christian it is much more; it is a ministry in which people of special capabilities can co-operate with God in the creative process by the establishment and maintenance of centers of holy affection.

A woman who takes the concept of a holy calling seriously will no longer demonstrate her deep sense of inferiority by trying to prove, on all occasions, that she is equal to men. Women, who are still affected by the vestiges of the feminist movement, have often claimed that men and women are just the same, in their intellectual and emotional achievements, but in this they have harmed their own cause. Their emphasis on equality has made them blind to the areas of their own superiority. A vast amount of common sense on this subject is expressed in Ashley Montague's much discussed magazine article, "The Natural Superiority of Women." Mr. Montague says what it is hard for a woman to say, but what is widely recognized, to the effect that women have superior talents, especially in the area of affection. "It is the function of women," says Montague, "to teach men how to be human." Nobody now subscribes to the ancient idea that women ought to confine their duties to the four walls of a house, but, in rejecting one error, we have tended to substitute another error for it. Between domestic slavery and the abdication of the mother there is surely a middle ground. This middle ground is what Mr. Montague presents so persuasively. He says:

It is, indeed, in the home that the foundations of the kind of world in which we live are laid, and in this sense it will always remain true that the hand that rocks the cradle is the hand that rules the world. And it is in this sense that women must assume the job of making men who will know how to make a world fit for human beings to live in.[2]

It is not only the mother for whom family life can be a vocation; this life is likewise a vocation for fathers, though necessarily and wisely in a different way. The man's right function in a home is less central than a woman's but none the less very important. The father must not act like a guest in his own home, but must share responsibility, including responsibility for those domestic duties involved in food and housing. He must take over part of the burden of necessary discipline, not leaving all the more unpopular tasks to his wife, while he comes on the scene as the generous benefactor. The Christian man will never look upon his home chiefly as a place where he rests between his hours of labor, but rather as the most valued enterprise in his life and one of the main reasons for engaging in gainful toil. In most human situations we have a combination of means and ends, but in a home the terminal aspect predominates. The good home, where people love one another and exhibit the divine pattern on a small scale, is the goal to which most other human activities point and for which they are undertaken.

A third guiding line is the loyal acceptance of discipline. It is the Christian teaching that men and women, if they are to fulfill their holy calling, must submit to a yoke,

[2] *The Saturday Review of Literature,* March 1, 1952, p. 28.

which means a limitation on self-centered freedom. We must reject openly and directly the modern heresy which encourages people to seek their own personal happiness, regardless of consequences. The person who shares Christ's yoke may, indeed, be gloriously happy, but he does not begin by asking *how* he can become happy. He begins by asking what is required of him as one engaged in a sacred calling.

The notion that our lives should always be easy and pleasant is not one that commends itself to intelligent persons. Everything worth doing involves both hardship and self-denial. Why should we think that the conduct of a home would be any different? Of course, the routine labor of guiding children's lives and keeping up a home involves many dull or even menial tasks. Of what work in the world is that not true? Of course, the woman who devotes herself to her children, when they need her most, is making some sacrifice, but the Christian answer is that we ought to take up the cross daily.

We shall be helped in the recovery of family life if we reject consciously the insidious pagan idea that men and women ought never to be inhibited. There is not a marriage that would last a week if all married persons were to follow the advice of giving full rein to all of their emotional urges. A man who is married is not, by that means, made impervious to the sexual charms of women, other than his wife, but he is engaged in a kind of commitment of life which, when taken seriously and devoutly, can enable him to rise above temptation. This may never be easy even to the end of the road, but it is not part of the gospel that life should always be easy.

A final guiding line is found in the idea of a home as a center of community service. The gospel, when taken seriously, constitutes a warning, not only against the breakup of the home, but also against the home as a selfish retreat from the world. We must always be concerned with our service to the world because we do not live to ourselves alone. A beautiful home in which the members are self-satisfied, while others live in slums, is no part of the Christian vocation. One of the chief reasons for establishing a good home is the hope that it may become a center of beneficent contagion, thus lifting the entire community.

Here is the middle ground between the self-indulgence of dispersion from the home, which is our present danger, and the self-indulgence of contentment in the home which was the danger of many of our forebears. Women ought not only to be the personal centers of homes; they ought likewise to use their homes for the service of the community and to employ their own increasing leisure, as life advances, for voluntary enterprises which are better done by concerned amateurs than by professional servants of the state.

There have been, in our history, brilliant examples of homes which were centers of new life, in that from them came new and liberating movements. Few examples are more striking than that of the home of Elizabeth Fry, who was a good mother, but from whose home came important developments in prison reform. We ought to glorify the pattern by which social vision is expected, as a result of home gatherings, and not merely as a result of gatherings of professionals or employed public officials. Thus the home may be one of the means by which the encroachment of the all-devouring state is resisted.

Though many young women, while their children are small, are terribly overworked, there comes a time in the average woman's life when she is amazingly and suddenly free. Some are so ill-prepared for this freedom from demanding responsibility that they go to pieces in the new freedom, pining for the old burdens, or spend the rest of their days in self-indulgent play or care of their own health. Since it is evidently part of the divine economy to give women the release which the end of childbearing marks, the part of wisdom is to use this freedom responsibly, as a precious gift. Older women constitute, in our contemporary society, our best approximation to a leisure class. It is well known that a true leisure class may produce some remarkably fine results in the advance of civilization. If women who are free from humdrum tasks would see their freedom as an opportunity to make the imaginative contributions which only a leisure class can make, there could be a new day for mankind. Now this possible gain is largely lost, not because we do not have the leisure, but because we do not have the idea. The loyal acceptance of the idea of a responsible leisure class would involve the beginnings of public work in the early years and its progressive increase, as domestic freedom increases, so that a sudden break may be avoided. Women cannot, in the nature of the case, perform two full-time jobs, but they can find increasing opportunity in the bits of marginal time which they have to give and this is wholesome.

Hope lies not in the denial of the home and not in confinement to the home, but in the employment of the home in the betterment of mankind. Both escape *from* the home and escape *into* the home are temptations to be equally resisted. The family ministry which we seek consists primarily in making of each home, first a demonstration of the Kingdom, and secondly a base for renewal in the larger community.

CHAPTER V

The Education of Laymen

A half way leap will prove as mortal as no leap at all.
LEWIS MUMFORD

THE idea of the ministry of the laity is a great idea, but there is no magic in it; it will not succeed unless it is undertaken with great care. There is no doubt that the layman often has a signal advantage in the ministry, as against the ordinary priest or clergyman, but this initial advantage will not carry him far unless he has something important to say and unless he learns how to say it effectively. Temporarily, at least, the nonprofessional man will receive a better hearing among some groups, notably in student audiences, but this will not remain true very long without something solid in the content of teaching.

We know that the stress on lay religion, important and revolutionary as it may prove to be, is no fool-proof solution of our problems, because amateur standing is not sufficient alone to keep a man from being inept. It is a good thing for lay men and women to share publicly in vocal prayer in services of worship, but the sad truth is that laymen may adopt the holy tone in praying just as easily as do some clergymen and, furthermore, the amateur is even more likely to put together a string of trite phrases without much reference to their meaning.

We have said much, and justly, about the perils of the religious professional, but we can say just as much about the perils of the religious amateur. Amateur preaching, at its best, is very striking, tending to win by its freshness, but, at its worst, it is often no more than a string of sloppily quoted Biblical phrases, linked by commonplace ideas. It is not easy work to think out an honest and consistent position in regard to God and man, and few laymen have had the time or opportunity to engage in a mature way in such an intellectual endeavor. Of course some clergymen have not either, but many have made at least a start, so that they realize that the problems are not simple.

The greatest danger which we normally face now, in the cultivating of the lay ministry, arises from an inadequate theology, especially one which is too self-centered. The beginner is strongly tempted to combine a stress on individualistic theology, devoted mainly to the saving of his own soul, with support of a conservative economic position. Sometimes he tends to identify the Christian cause with the welfare and interests of the financially comfortable and secure. Anyone who has attended many Christian conferences soon notes that the pastors are, on the whole, far more radical than the laymen in regard to economics and politics. This is largely the result of study, in that the average pastor has been stimulated by authors who, on Christian grounds, are deeply critical of the status quo, whereas the concerned layman, who has a keen desire to share his religious experience, may not have read even one such author. Often his only religious reading has been confined to the Sunday School lesson or to some conservative religious magazine. It is not his fault that he has not come into contact with more disturbing ideas, but it is a fact. Accordingly individual salvation, with very little insistence on social change, becomes his main theme. His theme is important and necessary, but it is not sufficient. Therefore, if the ministry of lay men and women is to be effective, in helping to produce the spiritual reformation which our time needs, we must face directly the weaknesses of the amateur and try to do something about them. We have, in the lay movement, a great deal of good will, but good will is not enough.

The obvious solution of our problem lies, in large measure, in the process of education. The revolt of the laymen will be abortive and inconsequential unless we can produce a far better training than most laymen now enjoy. It is important to get laymen ready to speak to laymen, because they often have marked advantages in this vocation, but there will be no short cut to success in the enterprise. One of the most surprising facts about the Christian cause today is the fact that so little thought has gone into the problem of how and where the ordinary Christian is to be trained, if we are to take seriously the idea of every Christian as one engaged in the ministry. It is obvious that the task is an enormous one, but, up to now, we have done little about it.

When the late Clarence Johnson, mentioned earlier in this book, decided, at the age of fifty-seven, to sever his business ties and to devote the remainder of his days to church work, he could not find where the training he needed was offered. He did not wish to attend a regular theological seminary, because he had no intention of entering an ordinary pastorate, and, besides, many of the professional studies expected of students in a seminary seemed irrelevant to his immediate prospects. He was told that he might join the young women who were training as directors of Christian education, but he hoped, instead, to be with those whose interests and experiences were more nearly akin to his own. Accordingly he went ahead with no training.

This experience is highly revealing. Our theological seminaries are numerous, whereas our training centers for the lay ministry are only beginning to appear. This is revealing in that it shows how little the New Testament idea of the universal ministry has been accepted or even understood. Now, fortunately, a change is setting in. If Clarence Johnson were alive today he could undertake the needed training at Parishfield, near Brighton, Michigan, or he could enroll in the new School of the Lay Ministry at Wittenberg College, Springfield, Ohio. It is possible that other developments, of a similar kind, may soon appear in various places, including Wainwright House, the layman's center at Rye, New York, where the subject of this chapter has been carefully considered already in a lay conference.

No doubt we can expect the use of many new schools of lay ministry as Christians begin to feel the importance of the idea, but such schools, alone, will never provide ?

full solution of the major problem. There are, indeed, a few lay men and women who can arrange to leave home or business early and prepare for full-time Christian work, but most people cannot do so, however intense their concern may be. Most training, therefore, will necessarily be conducted in people's homes or near them. This means that we must have a strong development of correspondence work, plus some way of fostering the group experience of those who engage in any serious plan of study.

It is at this point that the role of the pastor as teacher is of utmost significance. It is part of our shame that we have not used professional pastors sufficiently as teachers in our communities and particularly as teachers of theology. In almost every community there are well-educated pastors who have had a minimum of seven years of formal education beyond high school, usually four years of liberal arts and three years of theology, yet there are many communities in which these gifted and trained men are hardly used at all in the role of *teachers*. This failure is especially shocking when we know how nearly synonymous the words "pastor" and "teacher" are in New Testament usage.

The blame lies partly with the ordinary members, who have not asked their pastors to give them careful theological instruction, and partly with the pastors, who are willing to perpetuate the intellectual chasm between themselves and the members of their flock. It is not uncommon to find Christian communities in which the ablest lay members have no understanding of various points which the educated clergy take for granted, such as the documentary theories of the origin of various books of the

Old and New Testaments. Many pastors accept the scholarly conclusion that Isaiah 40, and following, is by an utterly different hand from that of the author of the earlier part of the book, yet they never share this revealing insight with those under their care. The consequence is that, frequently, what is said in the pulpit is understood in one way by the speaker, while it is understood in another way by the devout people in the pews. This would be less true if the pastor were to take seriously his role as teacher of theology to the local Christian community.

If we remember the New Testament doctrine of the Christian division of labor, the education of laymen will seem a perfectly natural part of the pastor's function. The pastor who understands his place in the Christian economy will spend a large part of his time educationally, both with individuals and with groups. He will guide individual reading, suggest books, encourage the development of speaking powers, train laymen in the vocal reading of the Scriptures, and guide the growth of devotional experience. When we contrast such a program with what the daily work of many contemporary pastors actually is, we realize that we are now wasting valuable powers. Many modern pastors, far from being the respected teachers of the Christian community, are chore boys, spending a disproportionate amount of time and energy as business managers. *They give their major time to tasks for which they have virtually no training, while they leave out those tasks for which they are elaborately trained.* If we should follow the suggestion of encouraging laymen, when they can afford to do so, to give up secular business and to volunteer as business managers of churches, one of the beneficent effects of this program would be the resultant freedom of educated pastors to use their time to educate others. At least this is one eminently practical means by which the time for teaching can be made available.

In recent generations the chief teaching in the Christian community, so far as Protestantism has been concerned, has been done in the Sunday School. The Sunday School is an institution so much taken for granted that we often fail to appreciate its true glory, but a little thought will make us realize both its actual and its potential worth. In some European countries, including those predominantly Protestant, the Sunday School, as developed in America, is not only unknown but is hardly believable. The notion that, in a single local church, fifty lay men and women will be teaching classes at the same time on Sunday morning seems fantastic to those who have never observed this phenomenon. There is probably no other single means by which we have developed the ministry of the laity so well. In the ordinary church service the lay men and women, unfortunately, often feel like mere observers, but in the Sunday School class, and particularly in the adult class, they feel like participators. This is one reason for the tradition, in some areas, which involves attendance at Sunday School and nonattendance at public worship. The people often like the Sunday School better than they do the church service because they have more responsibility for the conduct of the one than they have for the other. Insofar as this is true it ought to give us some insight into ways in which the conduct of public worship could be improved. We give lip service to the idea that we learn by doing, but often pay no attention to it when we come to our central religious experiences.

After we have said all that can truly be said about the glory inherent in the Sunday School idea we must go on to say that our failure to live up to its possibilities has been little short of tragic. There are thousands of men and women who have been members of adult classes for forty years, but in all that time have never followed a cumulative course leading to thorough religious knowledge. It is true that those who use the International Lesson material cover, in the course of a few years, a good many parts of the Bible, but the use of leaflets, rather than the Scriptures themselves, provides only brief and scattered glimpses of the possible riches. Many have been in a class for years without ever making a serious study of a single book of the Bible *as a book*. The division of the Bible into chapters and verses, which was no part of the original writings, provides facility of handling, but it also involves a serious handicap in that there is a temptation to think of the Bible in tiny units.

A completely new pleasure in study would come to many concerned Christians if they were to take a single book, such as the Gospel according to Luke, study its origin, its documentary background, its relation to the other gospels, its probable authorship, its relation to the book of Acts and its unique character. There is no reason why thoughtful and reverent adults should not engage in such study, precisely in the way in which it is undertaken in a first-class theological seminary, and there is no good reason why an educated clergyman, who has had the privilege of this rewarding kind of study, should not be the one to make it available to those under his care. If there has come to him a new understanding of the prophetic movement, by studying the prophets of Israel in the order of their appearance, so that the movement is seen as a cumulative development of insight concerning the nature of God and the nature of man, the pastor would be wise to share this approach, rather than stick to the almost meaningless order in which the prophetic books are ordinarily printed. If he understands something of how the Old Testament was put together, he will advise his students to begin, not with Genesis, which is one of the most difficult of books, but with Amos, the first of the writing prophets. All this seems obvious, but the truth is that there are countless churches in which no such educational program is followed or even proposed. Our shame is not that we have failed to live up to the Christian educational ideal, but that we have even forgotten what the ideal is. Our tragic waste has occurred, not because we could not reach a high standard in practice, but because we have so often been content with low aim. We have allowed thousands of adult classes to proceed on a trivial basis when they could have been the means, over a period of years, of remarkable growth toward an intelligently conceived end.

The success of the Great Books courses, stemming originally from the University of Chicago, has been an important revelation about what is possible. In hundreds of towns, groups of lay men and women, many of whom had done little or no serious reading for years, are now enjoying hugely the reading and discussion of the acknowledged classics of the race. Tired of the superficial articles of the average magazine and bored by modern novels, they have discovered wonderful satisfaction in reading Plato and Augustine and *The Federalist Papers*. Furthermore, in place of hit-and-run reading, even of the classics, many of the Great Books readers have undertaken to follow a cumulative program, several groups now being engaged in their sixth or seventh year of such study.

The chief revelation which has come from this program is the observation that many people can be attracted by a program which deliberately lifts the intellectual level, whereas their interest could not be held by the trivial or the easy. Perhaps it is really true that it is to do hard things that the humblest son of Adam dimly longs. In any case we shall be well advised, in the development of the education necessary to the health of the laymen's movement, to raise our sights and to keep them high. Some experiments have already demonstrated the wisdom of this program. For instance, on the campus of Stanford University, there was organized a class of fifty women, all mothers of school-age children, devoted to the scholarly study of the Hebrew prophets. The best books were read and the finest scholars, including Reinhold Niebuhr and James Muilenberg, both of Union Theological Seminary, New York, were used as special lecturers. The plan was to treat the women as adults, persons with full-sized brains, and to keep the intellectual level precisely as high as it ought to be kept in first-class graduate or professional

study. For this reason, more than any other, the plan succeeded famously.

This experience could be repeated in countless communities, with enormous advantage, if only we believed
in it. The existence of the thousands of women's clubs
ought to fill our minds both with wonder and with dismay.
Here are these great gatherings of eager human beings,
wanting to do something worth while and having the
precious time to do it, but the yearly program often adds
up to practically nothing. On one week there is a book
review, on another a talk on birds, on another an Armi-
stice Day program and so on through the year. If the
members should be encouraged to *study*, rather than
merely listen or be entertained, and if their study program
should be not only ambitious but cumulative, the results
might be beneficent beyond calculation. The clubs may
not be as bad as they were pictured in cartoons by the late
Helen Hokinson, but they point up vividly the tragedy
of waste, even more than the Sunday Schools do. We seem
to have a gift for making marvelous instruments and then
employing them for trivial uses. This may be a reflection
of our technological civilization in which the factory is
often far more exciting than is the product it turns out.

If the contemporary growth of lay religion is to fulfill
its promise, as the need requires, the chief subject of study
must be *theology*. The study of theology, which is concerned with the knowledge of God, is perhaps the most
mature discipline in which men and women can engage.
It is an exciting intellectual venture to use our minds,
with all of the honesty and integrity we can muster, to

try to work out a coherent system of belief, which is true to experience and in which there are no mutually contradictory elements. Obviously this is not easy and is not a task for children. Even the Bible is an amazingly mature book. Children can get something from it, but only those who have lived deeply and long and well can begin to understand its real significance. Theological study is more appropriate, therefore, for experienced persons than for the very young.

We have long followed the practice, in our Western culture, of allocating education to the earlier portion of life, with the result that many people never engage in serious study for fifty years after leaving school. It ought to be clear that this familiar pattern is based on a major mistake in the understanding of the human situation. Many subjects cannot possibly be understood by the young, though they may be understood by those who are older. The teaching of religion in college is made particularly difficult by the fact that most of the students have not yet lived enough to understand even the problems, let alone the answers. Most of them have not yet known the deepest joys or the deepest sorrows. Perhaps, if we were to become really intelligent about education, the greater part of the emphasis would be placed on the training of those of older years. *Education is really too good a thing to waste it on the young.*

We need a layman's theology that will help thoughtful men and women to face life's problems at the highest level. The tested rule is neither to underrate their *intelligence* nor to overrate their *information*. We must learn together how to answer such difficult questions as the following:

1. How is it possible to believe in the uniqueness of the Christian revelation without, at the same time, denying all validity to the teachings of the other world religions?

2. How is it possible to believe in the efficacy of intercessory prayer and yet believe that there is an objective order of natural law which makes scientific prediction of events a possibility?

3. Can we believe intelligently in both the goodness and the power of God, in view of the fact that so many innocent people suffer with such obvious injustice and without profit to themselves or others?

4. How can we believe in the evidential value of the widely reported direct experience of God when it appears that such experience is purely subjective or can be explained in psychological terms?

These are only four of scores of really difficult questions which our religion must face, but the sobering truth is that great numbers of serious believers have no idea of how answers that are both honest and satisfactory can be made. In this we are in striking and unhappy contrast with the lay evangelists of communism, who are so well trained that they have ready answers to the hard problems which are normally handed to them, and do not need to fabricate answers by improvisation. Of course, we shall never have perfect answers to anything, but ours is a fortunate time in that there has been an unusual amount of intellectual power employed in this field of inquiry with the consequence that the sting can be taken out of every one of these hard questions. What is so foolish is that we have not even tried, with any concerted seriousness, to bring the excellent theological thinking of our time to the rank and file of concerned Christians. Many have never even heard the names of such able Christian thinkers as Emil Brunner, H. G. Wood, John Bennett and Donald Baillie. The work has been done, but we have kept it under virtual lock and key, like the medical knowledge which is the unique possession of the physicians. To alter this situation is the next urgent step in the promotion of the Christian cause. We must produce more books which make the major answers understandable in language free from professional jargon and we must hand them to seekers as our ancestors handed out tracts.

It is helpful to try to envisage what some of the adult courses might be and to arrange them in a series, so that, at the completion of the series, the average lay minister would have a right to feel a certain competence in his preparation. One five-year plan, including courses designed for local churches and largely taught by local pastors, is as follows:

The First Year, The Hebrew Prophets.

This course would introduce many students to the scholarly study of the Bible, with documents read in historic sequence. The Biblical material would be carefully read in large units and studied with the aid of the best commentaries, including the *International Critical Commentary*. Older works like those of George Adam Smith would be mastered as well as contemporary interpretations. A useful procedure would be to read, during the year, the Biblical material in the following order, *Amos, Hosea, Isaiah 1-39, Micah, Jeremiah, Ezekiel, Isaiah 40 ff., Jonah.*

The Second Year, The Synoptic Gospels.

Each of the Synoptic Gospels would be read slowly, first Mark, then Matthew and finally Luke. The similarities and dissimilarities of the three accounts would be carefully observed, the chief documentary theories about the oral discourses would be considered and students might be encouraged to produce, with the aid of scissors and paste, their own harmonies, in three parallel columns. A general grasp of the life and teachings of Christ might be expected from this study, far more profound than anything known in previous experience.

The Third Year, The Christian Classics.

This course might follow the essential techniques of the Great Books Movement, but concentrate on acknowledged classics of Christian thought and devotion. Since this is a field in which the average Christian is even less at home than he is in Biblical studies, interest may confidently be expected to be high. A good method is that of using the full time of class for discussion of the interesting material already read, with little or no time given to lectures. A tested selection of books is as follows: *Augustine's Confessions,*

The Little Flowers of St. Francis, The Imitation of Christ, The Prayers and Devotions of Lancelot Andrewes, Pascal's Pensées, John Woolman's Journal and *The Prayers of Doctor Samuel Johnson.* This makes an exciting study for one year, all volumes being easily available in cheap editions, so that each student can own and mark his personal copy.

The Fourth Year, The Intellectual Understanding of the Christian Faith.

In this more mature study the class should consider all of the major and cumulative reasons for believing in God as well as the questions concerning God's nature and the Christian revelation. The hard problems, including those noted above, should be faced without hurry, and every effort should be made to arrive at a coherent system of belief. The reasons for believing in immortality and the doctrine of the resurrection should be handled *after* the other major subjects of the course have been studied.

The Fifth Year, The History of Christian Thought.

The greatest gap in the knowledge of most concerned Christians is the historical one between the Bible times and the recent past. Countless classes in Sunday School have studied various parts of the Old and New Testaments year after year, but very few have ever studied Christian history. The rise and decline of various heresies, the growth of the Papacy, the beginnings and completion of the Reformation, the origin of contemporary denominations, the con-

flict with science, all these and many more topics can
be exciting for both teacher and student alike.

Such a five-year plan may not be sufficient, but it
would provide us with something so much better than
anything we now enjoy that the results of following it
faithfully might be revolutionary in the growth of the
Christian cause. Those who would go this far would undoubtedly go farther under their own guidance or by
means of correspondence courses. Men and women engaged in such serious study could come together in summer conferences, not merely for random inspiration, but
for concentrated efforts to bring together the results of
their various studies. Those who have had the five-year
course ought, in many cases, to become the teachers of
others and some would probably be led to write in such a
way that they could communicate persuasively with other
laymen in their own language.

Such an ambitious program cannot succeed without
careful attention to libraries, both those of individual
Christians and those of churches. The idea that serious
religious books are to be read only by pastors is a heresy
that must be destroyed. The average Christian ought to
make the purchase of religious books an important item
in the family budget. Though the average church library
is a sad sight it need not be so. The supervision of such
a library is an excellent vocation for someone in each
local church and the person selected must be one who is
willing to do continuous intelligent buying. Several ex-
pensive works, which most individuals cannot normally

own, should be bought by the members jointly. A conspicuous example of such a work is the *Hastings Encyclopedia of Religion and Ethics*. If the education of laymen is envisaged as an important feature of church life, adequate money will be allocated to library uses. Church libraries ought to be open seven days a week.

The time of the week for the meetings of the theological classes is a matter of importance. It is agreed that we ought to lift the level of instruction in adult Sunday School classes, but it is doubtful if the serious study that is advocated can be done at that time, chiefly because the available period is usually too short. The average adult seminar ought to occupy at least two unbroken hours. The experience of some communities indicates that the best time for such study may be on Sunday evening, particularly when the students can attend as couples. The pastor who is willing to fulfill the vocation of theological teacher can often use his time more profitably in this way on Sunday evening than by putting on another service which is little more than a feeble copy of what was done in the morning. In some cases the traditional prayer meeting can be transformed into a serious educational venture.

Most of what has been said in this chapter has dealt with the intellectual aspects of faith, but this need not involve the neglect of the devotional life. One of the best services which the pastoral teacher can perform is in teaching people how to pray. Some Christian communities, in which this has been tried, report striking results in the lives of people who come to have a wholly new conception of religion when they become the persons who *do* the praying, rather than merely persons who *listen* while others pray. In this enterprise great gain can come from the promotion of layman's retreats, involving much devotion of time to silent meditation, from the formation of disciplined groups and from experimentation in new methods of group experience.

Great wisdom has been shown by a few pastors who have selected fifteen or twenty key laymen and gone with them to some conference center, miles away from their homes, for one or two days of concentration on their right vocation. The physical separation from the demands of home and business is essential to the success of this enterprise. One highly successful device, in such gatherings, is the practice of a group of ten or twenty sitting silently in the same room for a full hour, as each reads independently to himself the same section of Scripture which the others in the room are reading. It is the experience of numerous men and women that they grow more in one or two days planned in this way than is possible in a year of ordinary busy existence.

In all this we must keep the major emphasis, not on particular methods, but on the total enterprise. We are pointing toward high goals. We are concerned for the revitalization of the Christian movement, by bringing to its assistance a largely unexploited human resource, the ministry of lay men and lay women. If we try to do a little thing, we shall accomplish essentially nothing. Our only hope lies in making big plans, in undertaking to produce a radical change, in aiming high.

The ordinary airplane cannot move slowly! If it tries

to move slowly, it falls to the ground. In this lies the essential parable for our time, so far as lay religion is concerned. Unless we go much faster, the time may come when we do not go at all. Unless we take lay religion seriously we might as well save our energy.